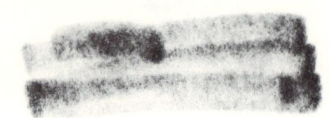

Simplified Quantity Regional Recipes

SIMPLIFIED QUANTITY REGIONAL RECIPES

Mabel Cavaiani, R.D. • *Muriel Urbashich, R.D.* • *Frances Nielsen*

Ahrens Series

HAYDEN BOOK COMPANY, INC.
Rochelle Park, New Jersey

TX
820
.C378

ISBN 0-8104-9453-1
Library of Congress Catalog Card Number 79-016623

Copyright © 1979 by HAYDEN BOOK COMPANY, INC. All rights reserved. No part of this book may be reprinted, or reproduced, or utilized in any form or by any electronic, mechanical, or other means, now known or hereafter invented, including photocopying and recording, or in any information storage and retrieval system, without permission in writing from the Publisher.

Printed in the United States of America

1	2	3	4	5	6	7	8	9	PRINTING
79	80	81	82	83	84	85	86	87	YEAR

Acknowledgments

The authors would like to give special thanks for help and encouragement in the preparation of this book to the following persons and organizations:

Della Andreassen, R.D., Consulting Dietitian, Lafayette, Louisiana

Donna Beckstrom, Director, Educational Materials Center, National Restaurant Association

Harold Blain, Administrator, Dry Pea and Lentil Commission, Moscow, Idaho

Mary Jane Chivers, R.D., Nutrition Instructor and Administrative Assistant, Christ Hospital, Oak Lawn, Illinois

Mary Agnes Jones, R.D., Chief Therapeutic Dietitian, Holy Cross Hospital, Chicago, Illinois

Frances Lee, R.D., M.S., Consulting Dietitian, Kerens, Texas

Yvonne Martin of Harshe-Rotman & Druck, Inc. for California Avocado Advisory Board, Newport Beach, California

Janet Hahn, R.D., Administrative Assistant, Patient Services, South Chicago Community Hospital, Chicago, Illinois

Roberta Freeburger, R.D., Nutrition Care, South Chicago Community Hospital, Chicago, Illinois

Staff of the Martha Logan Kitchens, Swift and Co., Oak Brook, Illinois

Members of the Armed Forces Recipe Service Committee

The American Dry Milk Institute, Inc.

The National Livestock and Meat Board

The U. S. Department of Agriculture School Lunch Program

CONTENTS

Introduction	1
Dietary Information	2
General Information	10
Menus	18

RECIPE SECTION

Soups	21
Meats	39
Chicken	69
Fish	87
Breads	95
Potato Substitutes	115
Salads	123
Vegetables	141
Sauces, Gravies, and Dressings	163
Cakes and Cookies	171
Pies and Puddings	189
Index	211

Simplified Quantity Regional Recipes

Introduction

There is a rising curiosity across the country today about the foods of other regions. Special foods are no longer confined to small areas. People hear, read about, and want to taste and enjoy the specialties of other areas and cultures. The rising popularity of regional foods may be a result of better communication, greater mobility, or a general increase in awareness of life about us; whatever the reason, the market is there, and it behooves the good food-service manager to take advantage of it.

Some regional foods are very complicated and time-consuming and not that popular with the general public, but there are many recipes—comparatively easy to prepare—which find great acceptance among the majority of customers. It is this type of recipe which we have tried to emphasize. It is obviously impossible in a book of this size to cover the specialties of even one region. Therefore, the authors have tried to choose recipes which they feel will have the greatest appeal to the largest number of customers. The following guidelines were used in selecting the recipes included in this book:

> *The recipe can be prepared with basic equipment from nationally available ingredients and will be acceptable to a majority of customers across the country.*

Dietary information is included with each recipe for the convenience of those nursing/convalescent homes, hospitals, and other users who need dietary information and do not have a dietitian available at all times. Dietary information is based on the basic recipe and should not be used for variations except as indicated.

Recipes in this book are suitable for nursing/convalescent homes, hospitals, cafeterias, schools, restaurants, and others wanting recipes for wholesome, nutritious, attractive, and generally economical dishes. Recipes have been simplified as much as possible for the use of cooks without much formal education in food preparation. Basic, simple equipment is used, and terms and measures are spelled out. Unusual ingredients are not used, and recipes which need to be prepared in small quantities are not included. Yields reflect generally acceptable portion sizes and can be increased or decreased if necessary, as noted in the chapter on general information. An extra column has been provided beside the *Weights/Measures* column of each recipe to record adjusted amounts. All measures and portions are level, and it should be emphasized that correct yields—particularly for meats—cannot be expected unless the correct temperatures and equipment are used.

It is hoped that users of this book will also refer to *Simplified Quantity Recipes (Nursing/Convalescent Homes and Hospitals)*, published by the National Restaurant Association in 1974 and written by the same authors, which contains several basic recipes that should prove useful to readers of this book.

The authors would like to acknowledge their debt to the Armed Forces Recipe Service Committee and the staff of the experimental kitchen at the U.S. Army Natick Laboratories, who compiled, developed, and tested the recipes in "The Armed Forces Recipe Service." Many of the recipes in this book have been adapted from that recipe service. Information from these sources has also been used: "Quantity Recipes for Type A School Lunches," U.S. Department of Agriculture, and U.S. Department of Commerce, National Marine Fisheries.

Recipes in this book may be used as a buying guide for food purchases. Meats, fish and poultry, canned and frozen fruits, and vegetables generally list the amounts to be purchased. (Most of the yields for meat, fish, and poultry are based on information in "Food Buying Guide for Type A School Lunches," published by the U.S. Department of Agriculture.) A table in the information chapter will also be of help in purchasing such items as carrots, celery, fresh green peppers, potatoes, and onions more efficiently.

Dietary Information

Nutrition information found at the bottom of each recipe is included as a guide for food-service supervisors who do not have a dietitian available at the time the recipe is used. The information pertains to the basic recipe only and not to any variations.

Information included is based on the *Manual of Clinical Dietetics*, published in 1975 by the Chicago Dietetic Association and the South Suburban Dietetic Association. Copies may be purchased from the National Restaurant Association, or from the authors, by writing to *Manual of Clinical Dietetics*, S.S.D.A., M.C.D., P.O. Box No. 425, Oak Lawn, Illinois 60454. The manual was researched and published by a committee of registered dietitians representing eight Chicago area hospitals. Information about recipes in this book may not always agree exactly with information in *Simplified Quantity Recipes (Nursing/Convalescent Homes and Hospitals)*, by the same authors, published by the National Restaurant Association in 1974, since that book was published prior to the manual.

The dietary information on each recipe is based on the following dietary principles.

General Diet

The general diet is designed to maintain or attain optimal nutritive efficiency, and forms the basis for all modified diets. It is to be used for adults who do not require dietary modification and, based on the individual's food choices, is adequate in all nutrients according to the National Research Council's Recommended Daily Dietary Allowances. In addition, women of childbearing age and children under the age of three need to include a major source of iron daily. The general diet should include the following daily selections of food from the basic four food groups plus additional foods needed to fill out the caloric requirements:

MILK GROUP
Children - 3 or more cups
Teens - 4 or more cups
Adults - 2 or more cups
  Cheese, ice-cream, and other milk-made foods can supply part of the milk

VEGETABLES AND FRUITS
4 or more servings
Include dark green or yellow vegetable; citrus fruit or tomato

MEAT GROUP
2 or more servings
Meats, fish, poultry, eggs, or cheese—with dry beans, peas, nuts as alternates

BREADS AND CEREALS
4 or more servings
Enriched whole grain
Added milk improves nutritional values

Soft Diet

It should be noted that food tolerances vary with the individual. This diet is designed for patients unable to tolerate a general diet. Fried foods, most raw fruits and vegetables, coarse breads and cereals, and highly seasoned foods could cause distress and therefore are eliminated on the soft diet.

Low-fat Diet

According to the *Manual of Clinical Dietetics*, this diet contains 40-50 grams of fat per day. Thus, all foods with a high fat content are omitted. Some fruits and vegetables which might cause gaseous distention may be omitted.

Low-cholesterol Diet

This diet limits meat, fish, poultry, or meat substitutes (except soybeans) to 6 ounces daily. Egg yolks are limited to 2 per week. Meats high in cholesterol and foods containing animal fat are omitted. The following guidelines should be followed:

- Not more than 2 egg yolks per week are permitted. Egg whites may be used freely.
- Skim milk instead of whole milk or buttermilk and yogurt made from skim milk.
- Margarine instead of butter.
- Duck and goose should be avoided.
- Shrimp should be excluded.
- Spareribs, mutton, frankfurters, sausage, bacon, and luncheon meats should be avoided altogether.
- Butter, rolls, commercial biscuits, muffins, doughnuts, sweet rolls, commercial mixes using dried eggs, and whole milk should be avoided.
- Lard or meat drippings should not be used. Oil or margarine should be substituted for cooking.
- Broths should be chilled and fat removed before they are used for soups or gravies.
- All visible fat should be removed from meat before it is served. Skin should be removed from chicken or turkey before it is served.
- Cream should be drained from cottage cheese before the cheese is served. Serve cheese which has not been creamed, if possible. Avoid other cheeses, except for cottage cheese or cheese which has been specially made for low-cholesterol diets. You may substitute 2 ounces of cheese for 3 ounces of meat.

Sodium-controlled Diet

The recipes in this book have been evaluated only for a diet of 2–3 grams of sodium, with foods high in salt omitted, as listed in the *Manual of Clinical Dietetics*. This diet is essentially a general diet with small amounts of salt used in cooking and none used at the table.

Bland Diet

This diet is the six-feeding bland diet in the *Manual of Clinical Dietetics*. Small frequent feedings are stressed with avoidance of fried foods, caffeine, alcohol, pepper, and highly seasoned food. Food tolerances will, of course, vary with the individual.

High-fiber Diet

The high-fiber diet is, of course, based on the general diet, so that any of the recipes would be acceptable. However, the general diet should include 3 to 4 servings of food high in indigestible carbohydrate. It is recommended that the high-fiber diet contain raw fruits and vegetables and more whole-grain breads and cereals with a high fiber content, with proportionately fewer refined breads, cereals, sugars, and sweets.

Diabetic Diet

The recipes in the book that might be used on a diabetic diet have been analyzed for their carbohydrate, protein, and fat content. All carbohydrate has been converted into bread exchanges or groups, all protein converted into meat exchanges or groups, and all fat converted into fat exchanges. In some instances, the carbohydrate is considered to be high for a diabetic diet, but the figures for the recipe have been requested by a specific ethnic group and so have been included.

Following are the food groups as listed in the *Manual of Clinical Dietetics*:

All Weights and Measures Are Based on Edible Portions

MILK GROUP 8 grams protein, 12 grams carbohydrate, 80 calories

	Amount Per Serving	Grams Per Serving
Skim milk	8 oz (1 cup)	240
Buttermilk made from skim milk	8 oz (1 cup)	240
Evaporated skim milk	4 oz (½ cup)	120
Nonfat dry milk, reconstituted	8 oz (1 cup)	240
Omit 1 fat serving for the following:		
Low fat or 2% milk	8 oz (1 cup)	240
Yogurt, plain, low fat	8 oz (1 cup)	240
Omit 2 fat servings for the following:		
Whole milk	8 oz (1 cup)	240
Chocolate milk (omit 1 bread)	8 oz (1 cup)	240
Evaporated whole milk	4 oz (½ cup)	120
Dried whole milk, reconstituted	8 oz (1 cup)	240
Yogurt, plain, made from whole milk	8 oz (1 cup)	240

FRUIT GROUP 10 grams carbohydrate, 40 calories
Fruits are fresh, frozen, or canned without sugar

	Amount Per Serving	Grams Per Serving
Apple, 2¼ inch diameter	1	80
Applesauce	½ cup	100
Apricots, fresh	2 whole	80
dried	4 halves	20
canned	3 halves	100
Banana, 6 inch	½	50
sliced	⅓ cup	50
Berries		
Blackberries	½ cup	70
Blueberries	½ cup	70
Boysenberries	⅔ cup	100
Cranberries	1 cup	100
Gooseberries	⅔ cup	100
Loganberries	½ cup	100
Mulberries	½ cup	75
Raspberries	½ cup	70
Strawberries	1 cup	150
Cherries	10	75
Currants	1 tablespoon	10
Dates	2 small	15
Fruit cocktail	½ cup	100
Figs, dried	1 small	15
canned	3	100
Grapefruit	½ medium or ½ cup	100
Grapes, blue, red, or black	12	75
small green seedless	24	75
Kumquats	4	60
Lemon, raw peeled	1 medium	125
Lime	1 small	100
Mango	½ cup	100
Melons		
Cantaloupe, 5 inch diameter	¼ medium	200
Cubed	1 cup	120
Honeydew	⅛	150
Cubed	¾ cup	120
Watermelon		
6 inch diameter × 1 inch thick	½ slice	150
Diced	1 cup	100

	Amount Per Serving	Grams Per Serving
Nectarine	1 large	60
Orange, 2 1/4 inch diameter	1 small or 1/2 cup	85
Papaya	1/3 medium or 1/2 cup	100
Peach	1 medium	100
Peeled and sliced	2/3 cup	100
Pear	1 small or 1/2 cup	70
Pineapple	1/2 cup or 1 large slice	70
Plum	1 large or 2 small	100
Prune, uncooked	2 medium	15
Raisins, seedless	1 1/2 tablespoons	15
Tangerine	1 large or 2 small	100
Fruit juices, Unsweetened		
Apple	1/3 cup	80
Apricot	1/3 cup	90
Cranberry, low calorie	1/2 cup	100
Grape	1/4 cup	60
Grapefruit	1/2 cup	100
Lemon	1/2 cup	120
Lime	1/2 cup	120
Orange	1/2 cup	120
Pineapple	1/3 cup	90
Prune	1/4 cup	60
Fruit juices, Sweetened with sugar		
Apricot nectar	1/4 cup	60
Cranberry juice cocktail	1/4 cup	60
Hawaiian Punch	1/3 cup	90
Peach nectar	1/3 cup	90
Pear nectar	1/3 cup	90

BREAD OR STARCH GROUP 2 grams protein, 15 grams carbohydrate, 68 calories

	Amount Per Serving	Grams Per Serving
Breads		
Bread, any kind, enriched or whole grain	1 slice	25
Bagel	1/2	25
Baking powder biscuit 2 inch diameter (omit 1 fat)	1	35
Bread sticks, 9 inches long	4	20
Bun, hamburger or hot dog	1/2 large or 1 small	25
Cornbread, 2 inch square	1	35
Croutons, plain	1/2 cup	20
English muffin	1/2	25
Matzo, 6 inch diameter	1	20
Melba toast, oblong	5	20
Muffin (omit 1 fat)	1	35
Pancake, 4-6 inch diameter	1	50
Popover (omit 1 fat)	1	35
Raisin bread, no icing	1 slice	25
Rolls, panroll or hard	1/2 large or 1 small	35
Rusk	1	20
Tortilla, corn or flour, 6 inch diameter	1	30
Cereals and Grains		
Cereal, cooked	1/2 cup	100
Cereal, ready-to-eat, no sugar coating	3/4 cup	30
Shredded Wheat	1/2 large or 1 small biscuit	15
Grits, cooked	1/2 cup	100

	Amount Per Serving	Grams Per Serving		Amount Per Serving	Grams Per Serving
Cereals and Grains (*cont'd*)			**Desserts** (*cont'd*)		
Rice, macaroni, spaghetti, noodles, and other pastas, cooked	½ cup	100	Doughnut, plain cake type (omit 1 fat)	1	30
Barley, pearl, dry	1½ tablespoons	20	plain yeast type (omit 2 fats)	1	30
			Gelatin, sweetened (jello)	½ cup	100
Crackers			Ice cream (omit 2 fats)	½ cup	70
Animal crackers	8	20	Sherbet	¼ cup	50
Graham, 2½ inch square	2	20	Ice milk (omit 1 fat)	½ cup	70
Oyster	20 or ½ cup	20	Puddings: cornstarch, tapioca, rice, bread (omit 1 meat)	½ cup	70
Round thin (Ritz), 1½ inch diameter (omit 1 fat)	6	20	D'zerta pudding made with skim milk	½ cup	70
Ry-Krisp	3	20			
Saltines or soda, 2½ inch square	5	20	**Flours**		
Triscuit	5	20	Arrowroot	2 tablespoons	20
Wheat Thins	12	20	Cornstarch	2 tablespoons	16
Zwieback	3	20	Flour	2½ tablespoons	20
			Tapioca, granulated	2 tablespoons	20
Snacks					
Popcorn, popped	1½ cups	30	**Vegetables**		
Potato chips (omit 2 fats)	15	25	Dried peas, beans, lentils, and soybeans, cooked (omit 1 meat)	½ cup	100
Pretzels, small	20	20	Corn	4 inch ear or ⅓ cup	80
twisted, medium	3	20			
Dutch or soft	1	20	Lima beans	½ cup	100
			Mixed vegetables	½ cup	100
Desserts			Parsnips	⅔ cup	125
Cake, plain without icing (angel or sponge)	1½ inch wedge	25	Peas, green	½ cup	100
Pound cake (omit 1 fat)	½ inch slice	30	Potato	1 small or ½ cup	100
Cookies					
Ginger snaps	3	30	Squash, winter variety (acorn, butternut, hubbard)	½ cup	100
Lorna Doones (omit 1 fat)	3	30			
Vanilla wafers	5	30	Sweet potato or yam	¼ cup	60

THE FOLLOWING VEGETABLES SHOULD BE COUNTED AS ½ BREAD SERVING

1 gram protein, 7 grams carbohydrate, 32 calories

	Amount Per Serving	Grams Per Serving
Artichokes	½ large bud	100
Beets	½ cup	100
Broccoli	½ cup or 1 stalk	100
Brussels sprouts	⅔ cup or 6-7	80
Carrots	½ cup	100
Green beans	½ cup	100
Kohlrabi	½ cup	100
Okra	8-9 pods	100
Onion, all varieties	½ cup or 1 small	100
Pumpkin	½ cup	100
Turnips or rutabagas	½ cup	100
Tomato	½ cup or 1 medium	150
Wax beans	1 cup	100
Leeks, 5 inches long	½ cup or 2-3	100

MEAT GROUP   7 grams protein, 5 grams fat, 73 calories

	Amount Per Serving	Grams Per Serving
Beef, veal, pork, lamb, liver and other organ meats, poultry, game, fish and shellfish	1 ounce	30
Canadian bacon	1 ounce	30
Luncheon meats	1 ounce	30
Pork sausage (omit 1 fat)	1 ounce	30
Frankfurters, 8-9/pound (omit 1 fat)	1	50
Cheese (omit 1 fat)	1 ounce	30
Cottage cheese	¼ cup	45
Canned fish	¼ cup	30
Egg	1	50
Peanut butter (omit 2 fats)	2 tablespoons, level	30

FAT GROUP   5 grams fat, 45 calories

	Amount Per Serving	Grams Per Serving
Fats		
Butter or margarine	1 teaspoon	5
Bacon fat and other meat drippings	1 teaspoon	5
Margarine, diet	2 teaspoons	10
Vegetable oil, lard, shortening	1 teaspoon	5
Miscellaneous		
Avocado	⅙	25
Bacon, crisp	1 strip	10
Cream, light or table, half-and-half	2 tablespoons	30
heavy	1 tablespoon	15
sour	2 tablespoons	30
whipped, unsweetened	2 tablespoons	30
Cream cheese	½ ounce or 1 tablespoon	15
Fat back or salt pork	1 inch cube	5
Gravy	1 tablespoon	15
Hollandaise sauce	1 teaspoon	5
Mayonnaise	1 teaspoon	5
Mayonnaise type	1 tablespoon	15
Salad dressing such as vinegar and oil, French	1 tablespoon	15
Tartar sauce	1 teaspoon	5

Nuts	Amount Per Serving	Grams Per Serving
Almonds	8 whole	10
Brazil	2 whole	10
Butternuts	3 whole	10
Cashew	5 whole	10
Coconut, fresh, 1 × 1 × 3/8 inches	1 piece	15
shredded, dried	1 tablespoon	8
Hazelnuts	6 whole	10
Peanuts	12 whole	10
Pecans	6 halves	10
Pinyon (pine)	1 tablespoon	10
Pistachio	20 whole	10
Walnuts	5 halves	10

VEGETABLE GROUP

Calories, protein, fat, and carbohydrate are negligible. If eaten raw these vegetables may be eaten in unlimited quantities. If cooked, 1 cup may be used per meal.

Asparagus
Bamboo shoots
Bean sprouts
Cabbage, all varieties
Cauliflower
Celery
Cucumbers
Eggplant
Greens
   Spinach, turnip, mustard collard, kale, chard, beet, chicory, dock or sorrel, watercress
Lettuce, all varieties
Mushrooms

Peppers, all varieties
Radishes
Sauerkraut
Squash, summer, all varieties (zucchini, crookneck, straightneck)
Water chestnuts

Limit per day:
   Tomato juice, 1/2 cup
   Vegetable juice, 1/2 cup
   Tomato paste, puree or sauce, 2 tablespoons

FREE GROUP

The following foods may be used without restriction.

Artificial sweeteners*
Baking powder
Baking soda
Fat-free broth, bouillon, or consomme
Carbonated or soda water
Carbonated sugar-free beverages with less than 3 calories per 12 ounces
Coffee: brewed, instant, or decaffeinated
Gelatin, unflavored or artificially sweetened
Herbs, spices, and flavorings

Horseradish, fresh or prepared
Mustard, dry or prepared
Onion salt, juice, powder, or flakes
Garlic salt, juice, powder, or fresh
Celery salt, seeds, or powder
Pickles, dill or sour
Pimiento
Poppy seed
Rhubarb, unsweetened or artificially sweetened
Salt, seasoned salt
Tea
Tenderizers
Vinegar

The following foods may be used occasionally without substituting. Not more than 1 tablespoon should be used per meal.

Ketchup
Chili sauce
Cocoa
Jelly or jam, artificially sweetened
Postum (cereal beverage)
Syrup, artificially sweetened

Worcestershire sauce
A-1 sauce
Soy sauce
Hot sauce
Lemon juice
Lime juice
Salad dressings, low calorie

---

*Consult with physician as to the use of artificial or low-calorie sweeteners.

SOUP GROUP

Each can of the following soups provides three servings so that one serving equals seven ounces. *Approximate Equivalents table is based on the addition of water to the concentrated soups.* If milk is used to dilute the soup, subtract the amount used from the daily allowance.

	Approximate Equivalents Per 7-ounce Serving
Campbell Soups	
Green pea	1 bread, 1/2 fat
Tomato	1 bread
Vegetable	1 bread
Chicken noodle	1/2 bread, 1/2 fat
Scotch broth	1/2 bread, 1/2 meat
Cream of celery	1/2 bread, 1/2 fat
Split pea with ham	1 bread, 1 meat
Consomme	Free
Beef broth	Free
Heinz Soups	
Green pea	1 bread, 1/2 fat
Tomato	1 bread
Vegetable	1 bread

	Approximate Equivalents Per 7-ounce Serving
Heinz Soups (*cont'd*)	
Chicken noodle	1/2 bread, 1/2 fat
Cream of celery	1/2 bread, 1/2 fat
Split pea with ham	1 bread, 1 meat
Consomme	Free
Beef broth	Free

	Approximate Equivalents Per Serving (4 servings per package)
Lipton Mix	
Onion	1/2 bread
Cream of mushroom	1/2 bread
Chicken noodle	1/2 bread

Approximate equivalents of convenience foods and foods not listed may be available from the dietitian.

General Information

Most of the recipes in this book were written to yield 50 portions. Since few kitchens serve exactly 50 portions and many recipes have a different yield than needed, it is often necessary to increase or decrease ingredients in a recipe. Because of this, a column has been left blank beside the "Weights/Measures" column in each recipe. This column is headed "For ___" and is for the users of this book to enter the correct amounts needed.

Contrary to what many persons believe, a well-proportioned recipe can be increased or decreased using the same factor for all ingredients. There is no need to increase or decrease disproportionately any one of the ingredients (such as spices or baking powder) if the original recipe is well balanced. However, it is important that all ingredients should be increased or decreased proportionately.

It is necessary to have a *working factor* to increase or decrease ingredients and yield of any recipe. A working factor is established by dividing the number of portions desired by the number of portions in the basic recipe. Most of the recipes in this book yield 50 portions. Therefore, 50 is the divisor. If the basic recipe yielded 35 portions, the basic divisor would be 35. If the recipe yielded 1 pan, as is the case of some of the molded gelatins, the total number of portions needed would be divided by the number of portions per pan to give the working factor, which would be the number of pans needed.

The size of the pan used in the original recipe can also be very important. If the recipe is changed, cake pans should still be filled about two-thirds full, each pie crust should have the same amount of filling as in the original recipe, and casseroles should be baked in deep or shallow pans according to the original instructions.

To Increase a Recipe

If 125 portions were needed, this procedure would be followed: 125 (portions needed) ÷ 50 (portions in basic recipe) = 2.5 (working factor). Since the working factor is 2.5, it will be necessary to increase every ingredient in the recipe 2.5 times. For instance, the recipe for Tomato Bouillon on page 38 would be increased as follows:

Ingredients	Weights/Measures × Working Factor		New Weights/Measures
Chopped celery	1 quart	× 2.5	2½ quarts
Chopped onions	1 quart	× 2.5	2½ quarts
Boiling water	2 quarts	× 2.5	5 quarts or 1¼ gallons
Chicken soup and gravy base	2 tablespoons	× 2.5	5 tablespoons
Beef stock	1 gallon	× 2.5	2½ gallons
Tomato juice	3 quarts (2 46-ounce cans)	× 2.5	7½ quarts or 1⅞ gallons (5 46-ounce cans)
Worcestershire sauce	2 tablespoons	× 2.5	5 tablespoons
Pepper	½ teaspoon	× 2.5	1¼ teaspoons
Salt	As necessary		
Croutons, chopped chives or green onions or whipped cream	As desired		

To Decrease a Recipe

If 35 portions were needed, this procedure would be followed: 35 (portions needed) ÷ 50 (portions in basic recipe) = 0.70, which would be rounded off to 0.75 to get a manageable working factor.

Working factors should generally be divisible by 2, 3, or 4 for ease in converting recipes. Therefore, 0.75 or 3/4 of every ingredient in the basic recipe would be needed. The soup recipe used to illustrate the preceding recipe increase would be decreased as follows.

Ingredients	Weights/Measures × Working Factor		New Weights/Measures
Chopped celery	1 quart	× 0.75	3/4 quart
Chopped onions	1 quart	× 0.75	3/4 quart
Boiling water	2 quarts	× 0.75	1 1/2 quarts
Chicken soup and gravy base	2 tablespoons	× 0.75	1 1/2 tablespoons
Beef stock	1 gallon	× 0.75	3/4 gallon or 3 quarts
Tomato juice	3 quarts (2 46-ounce cans)	× 0.75	2 1/4 quarts (1 1/2 46-ounce cans)
Worcestershire sauce	2 tablespoons	× 0.75	1 1/2 tablespoons
Pepper	1/2 teaspoon	× 0.75	1/3 teaspoon
Salt	As necessary		
Croutons, chopped chives or green onions or whipped cream	As desired		

To Adapt a Recipe

Since many recipes yield larger portions than might be needed, it is often necessary to adapt a recipe to the portion size required. In order to do this, it is necessary to know how many cups or ounces the recipe yields and how many cups or ounces are needed. For instance, if a recipe yields 50 portions of 6 ounces each, and 50 portions of 4 ounces each are needed, a working factor would be developed as follows:

50 portions × 1/2 cup or 4 ounces = 25 cups or 200 ounces (needed)

50 portions × 3/4 cup or 6 ounces (portion size in recipe) = 37.5 cups or 300 ounces

200 ounces (yield needed) ÷ 300 ounces (yield of recipe) = 0.67 or a 2/3 working factor.

This working factor would then be used to decrease the ingredients in the recipe as illustrated in the preceding table. If the recipe yields smaller portions than are needed, it would be increased.

It is also important when adapting a recipe to remember that the pan in which the cake, pudding, or casserole is baked is very important. Best results will be obtained when converting recipes by assuring the same depth of ingredients in the final pan as in the pan used in the original recipe. One of the easiest ways to do this is to calculate the square inches in the bottom of both pans and then develop the recipe accordingly.

Size of Pan	Yield in Square Inches
9-inch square	81
9-inch round	64
8-inch square	64
8-inch round	50
7 × 11-inch oblong	77
9 × 13-inch oblong	117
11 × 14-inch pudding pan	154
10 × 12-inch half steam table pan	120
12 × 20-inch steam table pan	240
12 × 18-inch cake pan	216
13 × 18-inch half sheet pan	234
18 × 26-inch sheet pan	468

Since an 18 × 26-inch sheet pan has 468 square inches of bottom surface, the same amount of batter which fills a sheet pan could be divided evenly among four 9 × 13-inch cake pans (468 ÷ 117 = 4). However, when the square inches of batter in a sheet pan are divided among 9-inch cake layers, the results are not as even (468 ÷ 64 = 7.3) which indicates that it will yield seven 9-inch layers a little thicker than the original cake or eight layers a little thinner than the original cake. In most cases the food-service manager would probably choose the eight layers to yield four 2-layer cakes. The amount of batter to be used in each pan can be calculated by dividing the weight or the volume of the batter by 8 in this case.

This principle may also be used when increasing or decreasing a recipe by developing a factor using the size pan for which your present recipe is written and the size of the pan which is to be used. For instance, if the present recipe yields 128 square inches (2 layers × 64 inches), it is obvious that it would yield a good cake if baked in a 9 × 13-inch cake pan (117 square inches), but if the final cake should be baked in a 12 × 18-inch cake pan it would be necessary to develop a factor by dividing 216 (square inches in a 12 × 18-inch pan) by 128 yielding a factor of 1.69, which would be rounded off to a working factor of 1.75 to increase the original recipe.

However, this does not mean that a home-sized recipe can be increased many times without failure. Home recipes are often out of proportion for use institutionally. They may have too much fat or sugar or liquid for a large amount and should be increased slowly, doubling and then redoubling them and making any corrections necessary as the testing progresses. However, a recipe which is in good proportion can be increased many times without failure and without changes in proportion.

Equivalent Measures

It is often easier when adapting recipes to use a smaller measure than the one used in the recipes. For instance, the use of cups instead of quarts or teaspoons instead of tablespoons will often make a recipe easier to convert. Measure equivalents to aid in converting recipes are as follows:

3 teaspoons	equals	1 tablespoon
1/8 cup	equals	2 tablespoons or 1 ounce
1/4 cup	equals	4 tablespoons or 2 ounces
1/3 cup	equals	5 tablespoons plus 1 teaspoon
1/2 cup	equals	8 tablespoons or 4 ounces
2/3 cup	equals	10 tablespoons plus 2 teaspoons
3/4 cup	equals	12 tablespoons or 6 ounces
7/8 cup	equals	14 tablespoons or 7 ounces
1 pint	equals	2 cups
1 pound	equals	16 ounces
1 quart	equals	4 cups or 2 pints or 32 ounces
1 gallon	equals	4 quarts or 16 cups or 164 ounces

It is also often important to know the equivalent measures of certain ingredients when recipes are converted. The following table gives some of the weights and measures used in this book:

Ingredients	Measures of 1 pound
Apples, bananas, or tomatoes	3 to 4 medium
Baking powder	2 1/3 cups (2 1/4 tablespoons per ounce)
Baking soda	2 1/4 cups (2 1/2 tablespoons per ounce)
Beans, dry	2 1/3 to 2 1/2 cups
Bran Buds or All Bran	2 quarts (1/2 cup per ounce)
Bread crumbs, dry	1 quart
Bread, sliced	16 slices
Bread, Pullman loaf	18 slices
Butter or margarine	2 cups (4 ounces per stick)
Catsup, tomato	1 3/4 cups
Cheese, shredded	3 1/2 cups to 1 quart
Chicken or meat, cooked and cubed	3 cups
Chocolate chips	2 3/4 cups (6 ounces per cup)
Cocoa	1 quart
Coconut, shredded	1 1/2 quarts

Ingredients	Measures of 1 pound
Cornflake crumbs	1 quart
Cornmeal	2¾ cups
Cornstarch	3¼ cups (3 tablespoons per ounce)
Cottage cheese	2 cups
Crackers, graham	60 to 65
Crackers, soda	82
Crackers, saltines	112
Eggs, whole	2 cups (10 medium)
Egg yolks	2 cups (24 to 28 medium)
Egg whites	2 cups (16 to 18 medium)
Sifted all-purpose flour	1 quart
Unsifted all-purpose flour	3½ cups
Macaroni	1 quart
Nonfat dry milk	3½ cups
Molasses or honey	1⅓ cups
Chopped nuts	1 quart
Noodles	1½ quarts
Onions or celery, chopped	3 cups
Peanut butter	1¾ cups
Raisins	3 cups
Rolled oats	1½ quarts
Long-grain rice	2¼ cups
Salad dressing	2 cups
Salt	1½ cups (1½ tablespoons per ounce)
Shortening	2¼ cups
Spices, ground	1 quart (4 tablespoons per ounce)
Sugar, brown, packed	2¾ cups
Sugar, powdered	3½ cups
Sugar, granulated	2¼ cups
Vegetable oil	2 cups

Nonfat Dry Milk

Many of the recipes in this book specify nonfat dry milk because it is easy to use, easy to store, and economical. Nonfat dry milk can be kept in its original container or in a covered container in a cool dry place along with other staples. It does not need to be refrigerated until after it has been reconstituted by the addition of water. It should be refrigerated after it has been reconstituted unless it is to be used soon. For general cooking purposes, nonfat dry milk should be reconstituted by stirring it into warm water with a whip. Whenever possible, the nonfat dry milk should be added to the other ingredients in a recipe and the water added as a liquid.

Children and older people particularly benefit from the use of nonfat dry milk because it can be used to enrich their food with additional protein, minerals, and calcium.

The following table of milk equivalents may be used for the substitution of nonfat dry milk in recipes which use liquid skim milk.

Nonfat Dry Milk +	Water =	Liquid Skim Milk
6 tablespoons	1⅞ cups	2 cups
¾ cup	3¾ cups	1 quart
1½ cups	1 quart, 3½ cups	2 quarts
2¼ cups	2¾ quarts	3 quarts
3 cups	3¾ quarts	1 gallon
1½ quarts	1 gallon, 3½ quarts	2 gallons
2¼ quarts	2 gallons, 3¼ quarts	3 gallons
3 quarts	3¾ gallons	4 gallons
3¾ quarts	4¾ gallons	5 gallons

Instant nonfat dry milk does not have the same volume as regular nonfat dry milk and cannot be substituted for nonfat dry milk on a cup-for-cup basis. If it is necessary to use instant nonfat dry milk instead of the regular nonfat dry milk, it should be done on a pound-for-pound basis using information on the package of instant nonfat dry milk.

Dehydrated Onions and Peppers

Dehydrated onions and peppers can be used in most recipes which specify chopped or sliced onions or green peppers. They are not generally used in salads but are excellent for stews, soups, and casseroles in which they need to be cooked. They can be added directly to the other ingredients when the recipe utilizes a large amount of liquid but they should be reconstituted if they are to be used in recipes such as meat loaves or many casseroles.

Reconstitution Guide for Dehydrated Onions

One pound (about 1½ quarts) dehydrated onions is equivalent to 10 pounds fresh onions as purchased or 8 pounds fresh onions which have been peeled and prepared for use.

To reconstitute dehydrated onions, measure onions and cover with twice their measure of lukewarm water. Let stand 30 minutes. Drain well and use as fresh onions. The volume will not be the same as fresh onions but the flavor will be the same.

Reconstitution Guide for Dehydrated Peppers

One pound dehydrated peppers is equivalent to 7 pounds, 4 ounces fresh green peppers as purchased or 6 pounds fresh green peppers which have been trimmed and are ready for use.

To reconstitute dehydrated peppers, cover with cool water and refrigerate 2 to 6 hours or overnight. Drain well and use as fresh peppers. The volume will not be the same as fresh peppers but the flavor will be the same.

Freeze-Dehydrated Onions and Peppers

Freeze-dehydrated onions and peppers can be substituted on a cup-for-cup basis for fresh onions and peppers since they don't lose volume as much as the regular dehydrated products do when they are freeze-dehydrated. Reconstitute either of them according to the directions on the package and use as fresh onions and peppers.

Purchasing

Efficient purchasing of food is very important in good kitchen management. It helps prevent leftover food and helps keep the cost per portion at a more reasonable level. Recipes in this book can often be used as a purchasing guide for meat and other items.

Efforts have been made by the authors to restrict the ingredients in this book to those which are available nationally, since it would be useless to include recipes which couldn't be prepared because the ingredients weren't available. If there are ingredients which aren't generally used, a local salesman can generally provide a good source for them.

A great deal of purchasing information is provided in the recipes, but items which are generally kept on hand such as carrots, onions, and celery do not have weights included in the recipes. Therefore, the following table has been included as an aid in purchasing those items. The table includes information regarding the yields you can expect when you purchase 1 pound of various raw fruits and vegetables.

Ingredient	Edible Portion in 1 pound as Purchased
Apples, whole	3 to 4 medium
Apples, diced for salad	2¾ cups
Bananas, whole	3 medium
Bananas, sliced	2¼ cups
Cabbage, shredded	1½ quarts
Carrots, chopped or sliced	3 to 3¼ cups
Celery, sliced	2½ to 3 cups
Cucumbers, sliced	2½ to 3 cups
Lettuce, whole	12 ounces
Lettuce, shredded	3 cups
Onions, chopped	2½ to 3 cups
Onions, sliced	3½ to 4 cups
Fresh green peppers, chopped	2½ to 3 cups
Potatoes, white, peeled	13 ounces
Radishes, trimmed	1 quart

Ingredient	Edible Portion in 1 pound as Purchased
Radishes, sliced	3 cups
Tomatoes, fresh, whole	3 to 4 medium
Tomatoes, trimmed	14 to 14 1/2 ounces
Tomatoes, sliced	2 1/2 cups
Turnips, peeled, diced	2 1/4 cups
Endive	1 gallon
Escarole	1 gallon
Romaine	2 1/2 quarts

Sizes recommended for food preparation in smaller institutions are given in the following table.

Item	Size of Package	Contents of Carton
Fresh Vegetables		
Cabbage	Crate	50 pounds
Carrots	Case	48 1-pound packages
Celery	Case or crate	1 1/2, 2 or 2 1/2 dozen per case or crate
Cucumbers	Basket	1 or 2 dozen
Endive	Per head	
Lettuce	Case	24 heads
Dry onions	Sack	50 pounds
Parsley	Bunch	
Fresh green peppers	Bushel	Bell, large, 10 dozen
		Bell, medium, 14 dozen
Potatoes, white, baking	Box	100 potatoes
Potatoes, white, boiling, etc.	Bag	100 pounds
Fresh Vegetables (*cont'd*)		
Radishes	Basket or bunch	30 bunches per basket
Tomatoes	Flat	
	(4 by 5, largest)	10 pounds, 1 layer
	(7 by 7, smallest)	20 pounds, 2 layers
		30 pounds, 3 layers
Fresh Fruits		
Apples	Box	100 or 113
Bananas	By the pound or by count	
Oranges	Box	113 or 88
Grapes	Lug	25 or 28 pounds
Frozen Vegetables		
Green beans	2 pounds, 8 ounces	12
Broccoli spears	2 pounds	12
Broccoli, cut	2 pounds, 8 ounces	12
Carrots	2 pounds	12
Brussels sprouts	2 pounds, 8 ounces	12
Corn	20 pounds bulk or 2 pounds, 8 ounces	12
Cauliflower	2 pounds	12
Lima beans	2 pounds, 8 ounces	12
Mixed vegetables	2 pounds, 8 ounces	12
Green peas	20 pounds bulk or 2 pounds, 8 ounces	12
Peas and carrots	2 pounds, 8 ounces	12
Chopped or leaf spinach	3 pounds	12
Mashed squash	4 pounds	12
Succotash	2 pounds, 8 ounces	12

Item	Size of Package	Contents of Carton
Frozen Vegetables (*cont'd*)		
Potatoes, French fried	5 pounds	6
Potatoes, shoe string	5 pounds	6
Frozen Fruits	10- or 30-pound cartons	

It is also important when purchasing foods to recognize the common can sizes, their capacity, and the number of cans packed in a case.

Can Size	Average Weight and Measure	Cans per Case
No. 10	6 pounds 8 ounces, 12 to 13 cups	6
No. 3 cyl.	3 pounds 3 ounces, 5¾ cups	12
No. 2½	1 pound 11 ounces, 3½ cups	24
No. 2	1 pound 4 ounces, 2½ cups	24
No. 303	16 or 17 ounces, 2 cups	24 or 36
No. 300	14 to 16 ounces, 1¾ cups	24
No. 1 (picnic)	10½ to 12 ounces, 1¼ cups	48
8 oz.	8 ounces, 1 cup	48 or 72

If it is necessary to substitute one can size for another, the following table can be used as a guide.

Can Size	Number of Cans to Use in Place of a No. 10 Can	Contents of Each Can
No. 3 cyl.	2	5¾ cups
No. 2½	4	3½ cups
No. 2	5	2½ cups
No. 303	7	2 cups

Frozen and canned fruit juices are a very important part of the daily purchases. Frozen juices should be kept in the freezer at 0° or lower, and canned juices should be kept in a cool, airy storeroom. Yields from juices can be figured as follows:

Type of Juice	Size of Container	Yield
Frozen Orange Juice (3 plus 1)	32 ounce can	32 4-ounce juice glasses
	12 ounce can	12 4-ounce juice glasses
Canned Juices (single strength)	No. 10 can	24 4-ounce juice glasses
	No. 3 cyl. can	11 4-ounce juice glasses

Measures

All measures in this book are level, and it is emphasized that the correct number of portions cannot be served from a recipe unless all serving portions are level. Weights or measurements, sometimes both, have been used for various foods according to the most commonly accepted unit of measurement for that food. The following rules should be observed for measuring ingredients to help insure the accuracy of the recipes.

Flour should not be sifted unless the recipe includes the phrase "sifted flour." There is a difference in volume in sifted and unsifted flour and the recipe may not give the best results if sifted and unsifted flour measurements are interchanged. Flour should be scooped lightly into a measure and leveled with a straight-edged knife or spatula. The measure should never be shaken to level it because this will result in a larger amount of flour than necessary for that measure.

Granulated sugar should be measured by filling the measure without shaking it and should be leveled with the straight edge of a knife or spatula.

Brown sugar should be rolled with a rolling pin before it is measured if it is lumpy. Brown sugar should be packed firmly into the measure and leveled with the straight edge of a knife or spatula.

Nonfat dry milk should be stirred lightly before it is measured. It should not be shaken to level the measure and should be leveled with the straight edge of a knife or spatula.

Baking powder, baking soda, and spices should be stirred lightly before they are measured. The measure should be dipped into the container and leveled with the straight edge of a knife or spatula.

Solid fats should be pressed firmly into the measure and leveled with the straight edge of a knife or spatula.

Dipper numbers are based on the number of level dippers in 1 quart. For instance, a No. 16 dipper is $1/16$ of a quart or $1/4$ cup. Ladle sizes refer to the number of ounces a ladle will hold. For instance, an 8-ounce ladle will hold 8 ounces or 1 cup. All measures are level. Some of the more commonly used dippers and ladles are as follows:

Dipper sizes

Number	Measures (approximate)	Weight (approximate)
60	1 tablespoon	1/2 ounce
40	1 1/2 tablespoons	3/4 ounce
24	2 3/4 tablespoons	1 1/2 to 1 3/4 ounces
20	3 tablespoons	1 3/4 to 2 ounces
16	4 tablespoons, 1/4 cup	2 ounces
12	5 tablespoons, 1/3 cup	2 1/2 to 3 ounces
10	6 tablespoons	3 to 4 ounces
8	8 tablespoons, 1/2 cup	4 ounces
6	10 tablespoons	5 ounces

Ladle sizes

Number	Capacity
1 ounce	2 tablespoons, 1/8 cup
2 ounces	4 tablespoons, 1/4 cup
4 ounces	8 tablespoons, 1/2 cup
6 ounces	12 tablespoons, 3/4 cup
8 ounces	16 tablespoons, 1 cup

Menus

Recipes included in this book are intended for the use of cooks in any part of the country to help them prepare recipes dear to the heart of cooks of other regions. It is not the authors' intention to teach Bostonians how to make baked beans or Southerners how to fry chicken, but to teach American cooks of all regions how to prepare and enjoy some of the foods of other regions.

It was impossible to include all of the recipes available. Many cooks across the country will probably feel that their favorite recipes were not included, and the authors can only say they are sorry. Space did not permit the inclusion of all recipes, so only the recipes which the authors felt would appeal to the greatest number of customers and residents could be included.

Generally speaking, it is expected that these recipes will be used by themselves to add interest to menus. However, if the occasion arises when more than one recipe of a certain region is needed, the first step would be to consult the index at the back of the book to see what recipes are available. Many American recipes which have been included have not been classified according to region because they are used throughout the country and they may be used with many menus.

The use of staples will vary from one region to another in the same country. The beans which are baked with salt pork and molasses in New England are baked with bacon and brown sugar in the Midwest, combined with rice in Georgia, cooked with tomatoes and onions in Texas, and boiled with bacon or ham in Kentucky and Indiana. Beans are used heavily in Mexico and our Southwest, where they are an important source of protein, but they are not as widely used in regions where other sources of protein are more available.

America is becoming a very mobile nation, and most Americans are familiar with the foods of the various regions in which they have lived or traveled. In short, we are becoming a nation of travelers, taking our likes and dislikes with us from region to region. The canny food-service supervisor or manager will sense this trend and be able to respond to the desires of customers or residents.

Recipes in this book have been simplified as much as possible and recipes which were thought to be too complicated have not been included. Spices have been adjusted in some cases, but those which have been included are important and should not be deleted unless absolutely necessary. Different regions use different spices, so it is wise to check on a specific spice before starting preparation of a recipe. The authors tried not to use any ingredients which were not nationally available, but in a few cases it may be necessary to order specific spices for a certain recipe.

The following menus have been planned within the framework of American menus. Regional menus are true to the foods of that region. These menus are intended only as illustrations, and it is hoped that managers and food-service supervisors will use them as a pattern for utilizing these regional recipes within the framework of their own menus.

New England Baked Bean Supper

Boston Baked Beans*
Fried Ham or Bacon
Cole Slaw*
Dill Pickles
Cornbread (Yankee)* with Butter and Berry Jam
Apple Pie or Cranberry Cheese Pie*
Coffee, Tea, or Milk

---

*The recipes can be found in this book.

Midwestern Harvest Dinner

Chilled Tomato Juice with Crackers
Roast Pork† with Cream Gravy*
Mashed Potatoes*
Applesauce
Corn on the Cob
Sliced Fresh Tomatoes
Relish Plate with Pickles, Celery, Green Onions, and Radishes
Assorted Soft Rolls and Butter
Fresh Strawberry Shortcake or Molded Fruit Gelatin with Sugar Cookies
Coffee, Tea, or Lemonade

Acadiana–Cajun Thanksgiving Dinner

Shrimp Cocktail with Crackers
Roast Chicken† or Turkey† with Dirty Rice* and Giblet Gravy*
Candied Yams†
Zucchini in Creole Sauce*
Buttered Green Beans or Peas
Fresh Fruit Salad
Assorted Hot Rolls with Butter
Fruit Cake or Banana Cream Pie
Coffee or Tea
Assorted Mints and Candies

Carolina Christmas Dinner

Chilled Fruit Juice
Roast Turkey† with Cornbread Dressing* and Giblet Gravy*
Candied Sweet Potatoes†
Steamed Rice*
Buttered Lima Beans
Fresh Fruit Salad
Spoonbread*
Coconut Cake or Lemon Meringue Pie
Coffee or Tea
Assorted Mints and Candies

Southwestern Saturday Night Supper

Vegetable Beef Soup† with Crackers
Steak Ranchero*
Hashed Brown Potatoes†
Creamed Brussels Sprouts with Celery
Fried Okra*
Assorted Relishes with Sliced Tomatoes, Pickles, Celery, Radishes, and and Green Onions
Cornbread (Arkansas)* with Jelly and Butter
Pecan Pie*
Coffee, Tea, or Milk

---

*The recipes can be found in this book.
†The recipes can be found in *Simplified Quantity Recipes (Nursing/Convalescent Homes and Hospitals)*, National Restaurant Association, Chicago, 1974.

Great Plains Sunday Dinner

Roast Prime Rib of Beef with Natural Pan Gravy*
Mashed Potatoes*
Buttered Whole-Kernel Corn
Molded Cole Slaw*
Assorted Pickles and Celery, Radishes, and Green Onions
Hot Baking Powder Biscuits* with Butter and Jelly
Apple or Pumpkin Pie with a Wedge of Cheddar Cheese
Coffee, Tea, or Milk

Northwestern Summer Dinner

Chilled Apple Juice
Baked Salmon Steak† with Lemon Butter
Baked Potato† with Sour Cream and Chives
Buttered Lima Beans
Avocado and Orange Slices on Lettuce with French Dressing
Onion Rolls* and Butter
Fresh Berry Pie or Bowl of Fresh Berries with Cream and Sugar
Coffee, Iced Tea, or Milk

California Summer Outdoor Buffet

Tomato Bouillon* with Croutons
Broiled Steak
Potato Salad†
Avocado Green Salad*
Buttered Broccoli or Cauliflower
Sourdough Bread or Assorted Hard Rolls and Butter
Lemon Chiffon Pie or Assorted Fresh Fruit and Cheese with Crackers
Coffee, Iced Tea, or Fruit Punch

---

*The recipes can be found in this book.
†The recipes can be found in *Simplified Quantity Recipes (Nursing/Convalescent Homes and Hospitals)*, National Restaurant Association, Chicago, 1974.

Soups

Baked Bean Soup (New England) 22
Lima Bean Soup 23
Bean Soup (Midwestern) 24
Catfish Gumbo (Louisiana) 26
Chicken Gumbo Soup (Southern) 27
Clam Chowder (Manhattan) 29
Clam Chowder (New England) 30
Lentil Soup (Western Style) 31
Menudo (Southwestern) 32
Okra and Tomato Gumbo (Louisiana) 33
Oyster Stew (New England) 34
Potato Soup (Midwestern) 35
Creamy Split Pea Soup 36
Creamy Salmon Chowder (Northwestern) 37
Tomato Bouillon 38

BAKED BEAN SOUP
(New England)

YIELD: 50 portions (about 2¼ gallons)
PAN SIZE: Heavy 3-gallon stockpot
PORTION SIZE: ¾ cup (6 ounces)
TEMPERATURE:

INGREDIENTS	WEIGHTS/MEASURES	FOR ____	METHOD
Baked beans or pork and beans	2½ quarts		1. Crush beans slightly with the back of a spoon. Put beans, onions, celery, broth, tomatoes, salt, and pepper in stockpot; cover tightly and simmer for 1 hour.
Finely chopped onions	1 quart		2. Taste for seasoning. Add more salt if necessary. (The amount of salt needed will depend upon the amount of salt in the beans and broth.)
Finely chopped celery	2 cups		
Fat-free beef broth	1¼ gallons		
Crushed canned tomatoes	3 quarts (1 No. 10 can)		
Salt	1½ tablespoons		
Pepper	½ teaspoon		
All-purpose flour	½ cup		3. Mix flour and margarine together until smooth; stir into soup; cook and stir over medium heat about 5 minutes or until soup is slightly thickened and has no starchy taste. Serve hot.
Melted margarine	½ cup (1 stick)		

DIETARY INFORMATION:
May be used as written for general and high-fiber diets.
Diabetic: This recipe provides 1 bread, ½ meat, and ½ fat exchanges per portion.
Low-cholesterol: Use beans which have been baked without meat in step 1.

LIMA BEAN SOUP

YIELD: 50 portions (about 2¼ gallons) **PORTION SIZE:** ¾ cup (6 ounces)
PAN SIZE: Heavy 3-gallon stockpot **TEMPERATURE:**

INGREDIENTS	WEIGHTS/MEASURES	FOR ___	METHOD
Dried lima beans Cold water	3 pounds (6¾ cups) 3 quarts		1. Pick over beans and remove any dark or discolored beans. Wash thoroughly with cold water; drain; put in stockpot and add cold water. Bring to a boil; boil 2 minutes and remove from heat. 2. Cover beans and let stand 1 to 2 hours.
Ham stock Diced smoked pork shoulder or ham trimmings	1½ gallons 2 pounds 8 ounces		3. Put ham stock (which has been chilled and had the fat removed) in the stockpot with the beans; add the pork shoulder or ham; cover and simmer 1½ to 2 hours or until beans are mushy.
Finely chopped onions Finely chopped fresh green peppers Shredded carrots Chopped celery tops Tomato catsup Pepper Salt	2 cups 1 cup 1 cup 2 cups ⅔ cup ¼ teaspoon As necessary		4. Add onions, green peppers, carrots, celery tops, catsup, and pepper to beans; cover and simmer for 30 minutes. Taste for seasoning; add salt if necessary. 5. Serve hot.

DIETARY INFORMATION:

May be used as written for general and high-fiber diets.
Diabetic: This recipe provides 1½ meat and ½ bread exchanges per portion.
Low-cholesterol: Delete smoked pork shoulder or ham. Add 1 cup (2 sticks) margarine in step 4. This recipe provides 1½ ounces protein per portion.

BEAN SOUP
(Midwestern)

YIELD: 50 portions (about 2½ gallons)
PAN SIZE: Heavy 5-gallon stockpot
PORTION SIZE: ¾ cup (6 ounces)
TEMPERATURE:

INGREDIENTS	WEIGHTS/MEASURES	FOR_____	METHOD
Dry white beans Cold water	3 pounds (1¾ quarts) 3 quarts		1. Pick over beans and remove any foreign matter. Wash beans thoroughly in cold water. 2. Add 3 quarts water to beans. Bring to a boil. Cover and boil 2 minutes. Remove from heat and let stand, covered, for 1 to 2 hours.
Ham stock	2½ gallons		3. Add stock (which has been chilled and had the fat removed) to beans. Cover and simmer 1½ to 2 hours or until beans are tender.
Finely chopped onions Thinly sliced celery Chopped fresh green peppers Chopped, drained canned tomatoes Chopped parsley White pepper	2 cups 1 cup 1 cup 2 cups 1 tablespoon ½ teaspoon		4. Add onions, celery, green peppers, tomatoes, parsley, and pepper to beans. Cover and simmer 30 minutes.
Diced cooked ham or ham trimmings Salt	1½ quarts (about 2 pounds) As necessary		5. Add ham to soup. Cover and simmer 5 to 10 minutes. Taste for seasoning and add more salt, if necessary. (The amount of salt necessary will depend upon the saltiness of the stock and the ham.)
All-purpose flour Cold water	1 cup 1½ cups		6. Combine flour and water and mix until smooth. Stir flour mixture into soup. Simmer another 10 minutes. Serve hot.

(continued)

DIETARY INFORMATION:

May be used as written for general and high-fiber diets.
Diabetic: This recipe provides 1½ meat and 1½ bread exchanges per portion.
Low-cholesterol: Trim all fat from ham in step 5.

CATFISH GUMBO
(Louisiana)

YIELD: 50 portions (about 3 gallons)
PAN SIZE: Heavy 5-gallon stockpot
PORTION SIZE: 1 cup (8 ounces)
TEMPERATURE:

INGREDIENTS	WEIGHTS/MEASURES	FOR ___	METHOD
Chopped celery Chopped fresh green peppers Minced onions Minced garlic cloves Bacon fat	1 quart 1 quart 1 quart 6 2 cups		1. Fry celery, green peppers, onions, and garlic in bacon fat in stockpot over moderate heat until tender, stirring occasionally.
Fat-free beef broth Canned crushed tomatoes 1-inch slices of okra Pepper Ground thyme Crushed bay leaves Tabasco sauce Salt	1 gallon 3 quarts (1 No. 10 can) 5 pounds 1 tablespoon 2 teaspoons 2 2 teaspoons As necessary		2. Add broth, tomatoes, okra, pepper, thyme, bay leaves, and tabasco sauce to vegetables. Cover and simmer 30 minutes. Taste for seasoning and add more salt if necessary.
Skinned and boned catfish cut into 1-inch pieces Hot cooked rice	10 pounds 1 gallon		3. Add fish to sauce. Simmer, uncovered, 10 to 15 minutes or until fish flakes easily. 4. Serve gumbo hot over about $\frac{1}{3}$ cup (No. 12 dipper) hot rice.

DIETARY INFORMATION:

May be used as written for general diets.
Diabetic: This recipe provides 1 bread, 3 meat, and $\frac{1}{2}$ fat exchanges per portion.
This recipe provides 3 ounces protein per portion.

CHICKEN GUMBO SOUP
(Southern)

YIELD: 50 portions (about 3 gallons)
PAN SIZE: Heavy 5-gallon stockpot
PORTION SIZE: 1 cup (8 ounces)
TEMPERATURE:

INGREDIENTS	WEIGHTS/MEASURES	FOR ____	METHOD
Chopped onions Chopped celery Chopped fresh green peppers Butter or margarine	1½ cups 1½ cups 2 cups 2 cups (1 pound)		1. Fry onions, celery, and green peppers in butter or margarine in stockpot over medium heat, stirring frequently, until onions are limp. Remove vegetables from fat with a slotted spoon and set aside for use in step 4.
All-purpose flour Crushed garlic cloves Hot chicken stock	1½ cups 2 2 gallons		2. Add flour and garlic to fat in stockpot. Cook and stir over medium heat until smooth. 3. Add hot stock (which has been chilled and had the fat removed before it was reheated) to the hot roux (fat and flour mixture) and cook and stir, using a wire whisk, over medium heat until smooth.
Crushed canned tomatoes and juice ½-inch pieces of frozen okra Crushed bay leaves Paprika Black pepper Salt Ground thyme Long-grain rice	3 quarts (1 No. 10 can) 1 pound (3 cups) 2 1 teaspoon 1 teaspoon 2 tablespoons 1 teaspoon 1⅓ cups		4. Add onion mixture, tomatoes, okra, bay leaves, paprika, pepper, salt, thyme, and rice to hot sauce. Cover and simmer about 20 minutes or until rice is tender.
Boned, skinned, and diced cooked chicken	3 pounds (about 2¼ quarts)		5. Add chicken to gumbo. Reheat, if necessary, and serve hot.

(continued)

DIETARY INFORMATION:

May be used as written for general diets.
Diabetic: This recipe provides 1 meat and 1½ fat exchanges per portion.
Low-cholesterol: Use margarine in step 1.
This recipe provides 1 ounce protein per portion.

CLAM CHOWDER
(Manhattan)

YIELD: 50 portions (about 3 gallons)
PAN SIZE: Heavy 5-gallon stockpot
PORTION SIZE: 1 cup (8 ounces)
TEMPERATURE:

INGREDIENTS	WEIGHTS/MEASURES	FOR ____	METHOD
Chopped bacon Chopped onions Diced celery Chopped fresh green peppers	8 ounces 3 cups 3 cups 2 cups		1. Fry bacon over moderate heat in heavy frying pan, stirring occasionally, until crisp; remove to stockpot with slotted spoon. 2. Fry onions, celery, and green peppers in bacon fat until onions are golden; remove with slotted spoon to stockpot.
Chopped canned clams Water	3 quarts (6 pounds) As necessary		3. Drain clams and keep for use in step 5. Add water to clam juice to yield 1½ gallons liquid and put in stockpot.
Canned crushed tomatoes Diced carrots Salt Pepper Ground thyme Diced fresh white potatoes	3 quarts (1 No. 10 can) 2 cups 2 tablespoons 1½ teaspoons 1 teaspoon 2 quarts		4. Add tomatoes, carrots, salt, pepper, thyme, and potatoes to stockpot. Cover and simmer 20 to 30 minutes or until vegetables are tender. 5. Add drained clams to chowder. Cover and simmer 5 minutes. Serve hot.

DIETARY INFORMATION:

May be used as written for general, high-fiber, and mild 2-to-3-gram sodium-restricted diets.
Diabetic: This recipe provides ½ bread, 2 meat, and ½ fat exchanges per portion.
Low-cholesterol: Substitute ½ cup vegetable oil for bacon fat in step 1.
This recipe provides 2 ounces protein per portion.

NOTES:

Variation:
MANHATTAN FISH CHOWDER: Use 6 pounds skinless fish fillets cut in 2-inch pieces and 1½ gallons water instead of clams and clam juice in step 3. Add fish to water; cover and simmer 20 minutes. Proceed with step 4 in basic recipe.

CLAM CHOWDER
(New England)

YIELD: 50 portions (about 3 gallons)   **PORTION SIZE:** 1 cup (8 ounces)
PAN SIZE: Heavy 5-gallon stockpot   **TEMPERATURE:**

INGREDIENTS	WEIGHTS/MEASURES	FOR ____	METHOD
Chopped canned clams Water Diced fresh white potatoes	3 quarts (6 pounds) As necessary 2 quarts		1. Drain clams and save for use in step 4. Add water to clam juice to yield 1 gallon liquid. Put liquid and potatoes in stockpot. Cover and simmer 20 minutes or until potatoes are tender.
Diced bacon Chopped onions Butter or margarine All purpose flour	8 ounces 1 quart 1½ cups (3 sticks) 2 cups		2. Fry bacon in heavy frying pan over low heat, stirring frequently, until bacon is crisp. Remove bacon to stockpot with a slotted spoon. 3. Fry onions in bacon fat over moderate heat, stirring occasionally, until onions are golden. Add butter or margarine to onions; stir over low heat until melted; add flour and cook and stir until smooth. Cool.
Nonfat dry milk Hot water Salt Black pepper	1½ quarts 1½ gallons 3 tablespoons 1 teaspoon		4. Blend dry milk into water and add with clams to potatoes. Add flour mixture to chowder. Cook and stir over moderate heat until smooth. Reduce heat and simmer, stirring occasionally, about 30 minutes longer to allow chowder to thicken and develop flavor. 5. Add salt and pepper to chowder and serve hot.

DIETARY INFORMATION:

May be used as written for general diets.
Diabetic: This recipe provides 1½ bread, ½ meat, and 1 fat exchanges per portion.
Low-cholesterol: Use ½ cup vegetable oil instead of bacon in step 2 and use margarine in step 3. This recipe provides 1 ounce protein per portion.

NOTES:

Variation:
NEW ENGLAND FISH CHOWDER: Use 6 pounds of skinless fish fillets cut into 2-inch pieces and 1 gallon of water instead of the clams and juice in step 1.

LENTIL SOUP
(Western Style)

YIELD: 50 portions (about 3 gallons)
PAN SIZE: Heavy 5-gallon stockpot
PORTION SIZE: 1 cup (8 ounces)
TEMPERATURE:

INGREDIENTS	WEIGHTS/MEASURES	FOR _____	METHOD
Chopped bacon	1 pound		1. Fry bacon over low heat in heavy frying pan, stirring frequently, until bacon is crisp; remove bacon to stockpot with a slotted spoon.
Chopped onions Chopped celery Chopped fresh green peppers	3 cups 1 quart 3 cups		2. Fry onions, celery, and green peppers in hot bacon fat over medium heat, stirring occasionally, until onions are golden; remove vegetables to stockpot with a slotted spoon.
Hot ham stock Ham bone Dried lentils Catsup Molasses Brown sugar Vinegar Dry mustard Liquid smoke Tabasco sauce Salt	3 gallons 1 6 pounds (about 3½ quarts) 2 cups ½ cup ½ cup ½ cup 1 tablespoon 1 tablespoon 1 teaspoon As necessary		3. Put hot ham stock (which has been chilled and had the fat removed) in the stockpot with the ham bone, lentils, catsup, molasses, brown sugar, vinegar, mustard, liquid smoke, and tabasco sauce; cover and simmer 2 hours or until lentils are tender. Taste for seasoning and add more salt, if necessary. Remove ham bone. 4. Serve hot.

DIETARY INFORMATION:

May be used as written for general and high-fiber diets.
Diabetic: This recipe provides 2½ bread, 2 meat, and 1 fat exchanges per portion.
This recipe provides 2 ounces of protein per portion.

MENUDO
(Southwestern)

YIELD: 50 portions (about 3 gallons) **PORTION SIZE:** 1 cup (8 ounces)
PAN SIZE: Heavy 5-gallon stockpot **TEMPERATURE:**

INGREDIENTS	WEIGHTS/MEASURES	FOR ___	METHOD
Tripe Water	15 pounds 3 gallons		1. Place tripe and water in stockpot. Cover and simmer about 2 hours or until tender. Cool. Skim fat from liquid. Remove tripe from liquid and cut into cubes. Return tripe to pot.
Canned drained hominy Chopped onions Salt Garlic powder Pepper Chili powder Oregano	3 quarts (1 No. 10 can) 1 quart 2 teaspoons 1 teaspoon 1 teaspoon 3 tablespoons 1 tablespoon		2. Add hominy, onions, salt, garlic, pepper, chili powder, and oregano to tripe. Cover and simmer 20 minutes or until onions are tender.
Chopped green onions and tops	2 cups		3. Serve hot soup garnished with a heaping teaspoonful of onions.

DIETARY INFORMATION:

May be used as written for general, high-protein, low-cholesterol, and 2-to-3-gram mild sodium-restricted diets.
Diabetic: This recipe provides 2 bread, 4 meat, and ½ fat exchanges per portion.
This recipe provides 4 ounces protein per portion.

NOTES: This recipe was furnished by Arma B. Page who was chief nutrition therapy education and research dietitian at Brentwood V.A. Hospital in Los Angeles, California, before her retirement. Mrs. Page said that while this recipe is often featured in homes and restaurants during the holidays, it is also eaten throughout the year for breakfast and especially on Sundays. It is said to be good for hangovers if the fat is not removed from the soup.

OKRA AND TOMATO GUMBO
(Louisiana)

YIELD: 50 portions (about 1½ gallons)
PAN SIZE: Heavy 3-gallon stockpot
PORTION SIZE: ½ cup
TEMPERATURE:

INGREDIENTS	WEIGHTS/MEASURES	FOR _____	METHOD
Chopped onions Chopped bacon	3 cups 8 ounces		1. Fry onions and bacon together over moderate heat in stockpot, stirring occasionally, until onions are lightly browned.
1-inch slices of okra	5 pounds		2. Add okra to onions and bacon. Cook, stirring frequently, over moderate heat for another 5 minutes.
All purpose flour Sugar Salt Paprika Red pepper Ground oregano Pepper Canned crushed tomatoes Boiling water	½ cup 2 tablespoons 1½ tablespoons 1 tablespoon 1 teaspoon 1 teaspoon ½ teaspoon 3 quarts (1 No. 10 can) 2 cups		3. Stir flour, sugar, salt, paprika, red pepper, oregano, and pepper together and add to vegetables. Stir until blended. 4. Add tomatoes and water to vegetables. Mix well. Cover and simmer 15 minutes or until okra is tender.
Hot cooked rice	1 gallon		5. Serve gumbo over about ⅓ cup (No. 12 dipper) hot rice.

DIETARY INFORMATION:

May be used as written for general diets.
Diabetic: This recipe provides 1 bread and ½ fat exchanges per portion.

OYSTER STEW
(New England)

YIELD: 50 portions (about 3 gallons)
PAN SIZE: Heavy 5-gallon stockpot
PORTION SIZE: 1 cup (8 ounces)
TEMPERATURE:

INGREDIENTS	WEIGHTS/MEASURES	FOR ___	METHOD
Oysters and liquid	9 pounds (1½ gallons)		1. Remove any pieces of shell from oysters. 2. Cook oysters in their own liquid over low heat, stirring constantly, until the edges of the oysters begin to curl.
Nonfat dry milk Hot water	1½ quarts 1½ gallons		3. Combine dry milk and hot water in stockpot. Heat to just below boiling. Do not boil.
Butter or margarine Salt Pepper Coffee cream (18%)	2 cups (1 pound) 3 tablespoons 1 teaspoon 2 quarts		4. Add butter or margarine, salt, pepper, and cream to milk. Mix lightly. 5. Add hot oysters with their liquid to hot milk mixture. Mix lightly and serve immediately.

DIETARY INFORMATION:

May be used as written for general and soft diets.
Low-cholesterol: Stir 1 cup nonfat dry milk into 1 quart skim milk and use instead of cream in step 4. Use margarine in step 4.
This recipe provides 1 ounce protein per portion.

NOTES:

Variation:
SCALLOP STEW: Omit oysters. Use 8 pounds halved or quartered scallops, 2 pounds skinned and chopped fish fillets, and 1½ quarts cold water instead of oysters and oyster liquid in step 2. Simmer scallops, fish, and water, covered, over low heat for 15 minutes or until scallops and fish flake easily. Add to hot liquid in step 5 instead of oysters and liquid. Serve immediately.

POTATO SOUP
(Midwestern)

YIELD: 50 portions (about 2½ gallons)
PAN SIZE: Heavy 5-gallon stockpot
PORTION SIZE: ¾ cup (6 ounces)
TEMPERATURE:

INGREDIENTS	WEIGHTS/MEASURES	FOR ___	METHOD
Diced fresh white potatoes Boiling water Salt Whole milk	3 quarts 3 quarts 3 tablespoons As necessary		1. Cook potatoes, water, and salt together in covered pot about 15 minutes or until potatoes are tender. 2. Drain potatoes. Add enough milk to potato water to total 2 gallons.
Finely chopped onions Finely chopped celery Butter or margarine	1½ cups ½ cup 1 cup (2 sticks)		3. Fry onions and celery in butter or margarine in stockpot over medium heat, stirring frequently, until onions are transparent. Do not allow them to brown.
All-purpose flour White pepper	¾ cup 1 teaspoon		4. Stir flour and pepper into onion mixture. Cook and stir over medium heat until smooth but not browned. Add warm milk to onion mixture. Cook, stirring constantly, over medium heat, until smooth and the starchy taste is gone.
Coffee cream (18%)	1 quart		5. Add cream and potatoes to hot sauce. Reheat to serving temperature, if necessary, and serve hot.

DIETARY INFORMATION:

May be used as written for general diets.
Low-cholesterol: Use skim milk in step 2 and margarine in step 3. Stir 1 cup of nonfat dry milk into 1 quart skim milk and use instead of coffee cream in step 5.

CREAMY SPLIT PEA SOUP

YIELD: 50 portions (about 2¼ gallons)
PAN SIZE: Heavy 3-gallon stockpot

PORTION SIZE: ¾ cup (6 ounces)
TEMPERATURE:

INGREDIENTS	WEIGHTS/MEASURES	FOR ___	METHOD
Dry split peas Cold water	3 pounds (1½ quarts) 2 gallons		1. Pick over peas and remove any foreign matter. Wash thoroughly with cold water; drain. Put in stockpot and add cold water. Bring to a boil; boil 2 minutes and remove from heat. 2. Cover and let stand 1½ to 2 hours.
Chopped onions Chopped celery and leaves Chopped carrots Chopped parsley Salt Pepper Bay leaf Ground thyme Garlic salt	1 quart 1 quart 1 cup 1 tablespoon 2 tablespoons ½ teaspoon 1 1 teaspoon 1 tablespoon		3. Add onions, celery and leaves, carrots, parsley, salt, pepper, bay leaf, thyme, and garlic salt to peas; cover and simmer 1½ to 2 hours or until peas are mushy. Taste soup for seasoning; add more salt, if necessary.
Coffee cream (18%) Chopped bacon, chopped egg or croutons (optional)	2 quarts As necessary		4. Stir cream into soup. Reheat to serving temperature, if necessary. Serve hot garnished with chopped bacon, chopped eggs, or croutons, or serve plain.

DIETARY INFORMATION:

May be used as written for general and high-fiber diets.
Diabetic: This recipe provides 1½ bread, 1 meat, and 1½ fat exchanges per portion.
Low-cholesterol: Garnish with croutons or serve plain and substitute 3 cups of nonfat dry milk dissolved in 2 quarts of warm water for the 2 quarts of coffee cream.
This recipe provides 1 ounce of protein per portion.

CREAMY SALMON CHOWDER
(Northwestern)

YIELD: 50 portions (about 3 gallons)
PAN SIZE: Heavy 5-gallon stockpot
PORTION SIZE: 1 cup (8 ounces)
TEMPERATURE:

INGREDIENTS	WEIGHTS/MEASURES	FOR ___	METHOD
Canned salmon	4 pounds (1 4-pound can)		1. Drain salmon. Keep juice for use in step 2. Discard skin and bones. Refrigerate salmon for use in step 4, after it has been broken into pieces.
Chicken stock Diced onions Diced fresh white potatoes Diced instant sweet red or green peppers Thinly sliced celery Salt White pepper	As necessary 1 quart 2 quarts 1 cup 1 cup 2 tablespoons ½ teaspoon		2. Add chicken stock (which has been chilled and had the fat removed) to the salmon juice to equal 2 gallons. Place in stockpot with onions, potatoes, dry peppers, celery, salt, and pepper. Cover and simmer 15 to 20 minutes or until vegetables are tender.
Instant dry potatoes Coffee cream (18%) Chopped parsley (optional)	1 quart 2 quarts As desired		3. Add potatoes to chowder, stirring constantly. Simmer 1 or 2 minutes. 4. Stir salmon and cream into soup. Reheat to serving temperature. Serve hot, garnished with parsley, if desired.

DIETARY INFORMATION:

May be used as written for general diets.
Low-cholesterol: Use fat-free chicken stock in step 2 and stir 1 cup nonfat dry milk into 1 quart skim milk and use instead of cream in step 4.
This recipe provides 1 ounce protein per portion.

TOMATO BOUILLON

YIELD: 50 portions (about 2¼ gallons)
PAN SIZE: Heavy 3-gallon stockpot
PORTION SIZE: ¾ cup (6 ounces)
TEMPERATURE:

INGREDIENTS	WEIGHTS/MEASURES	FOR ___	METHOD
Chopped celery Chopped onions Boiling water Chicken soup and gravy mix	1 quart 1 quart 2 quarts 2 tablespoons		1. Combine celery, onions, water, and soup and gravy base. Cover and simmer 30 minutes or until vegetables are very tender. Strain broth; discard vegetables and return broth to stockpot.
Beef stock Tomato juice Worcestershire sauce Pepper Salt Croutons, chopped chives or whipped cream	1 gallon 3 quarts (2 46-ounce cans) 2 tablespoons ½ teaspoon As necessary As desired		2. Add beef stock, tomato juice, Worcestershire sauce and pepper to broth in stockpot. Heat to serving temperature. Taste for seasoning. Add salt if necessary. Serve hot, garnished with croutons, chopped chives or green onions or whipped cream.

DIETARY INFORMATION:

May be used as written for general diets.
Diabetic: This recipe provides ½ bread exchange per portion.
Low-cholesterol: Use fat-free broth and garnish with croutons, chopped chives, or onions.

Meats

Beef
    Beef Pasties (Northern Michigan) 42
    Boiled Dinner (New England) 44
    Chili (Chicago) 46
        Chili-Mac 47
        Chili with Rice 47
    Chili (Texas) 48
    Hot Spiced Corned Beef Sandwiches (Midwestern) 50
    Creole Macaroni (Southern) 51
    Enchiladas (Southwestern) 53
    Martha's Company Casserole 55
    Meat Loaf 56
    Argo Meat Loaf 57
        Meat Loaf (Midwestern) 57
    Reuben Sandwiches 58
    Roast Beef Hash 59
    Steak Ranchero (Southwestern) 61
    Tacos (Southwestern) 62
    Tostados (Southwestern) 63

Lamb
    Broiled Lamb Patties 64

Pork
    Simmered Chitterlings 65
        Deep Fat Fried Chitterlings 65
    Ham Loaf 66
    Pork Chops in Apricot Sauce (California) 67
    Simmered Pork Hocks 68
        Simmered Pigs' Feet 68

Information

Many regional recipes specify the less expensive cuts of meat because seldom in the history of the world has the amount and variety of meat been available to everyone as it is now in our country. It is the slowly simmered stew, the ground meats extended with vegetables and starches, and the variety meats which are remembered. These were the memories of the people who emigrated to this country and it is these recipes prepared with loving care and memories of their homelands which we remember and enjoy now.

The early immigrants developed recipes using the food available to them in this country and it is these regional recipes which we have used in this book. It is regrettable that it was impossible to cover all of the recipes available, but that would take many books and, therefore, the authors have had to pick and choose among recipes which they thought would appeal to most Americans. Every effort has been made to keep the recipes as true to their origins as possible while still using modern ingredients and preparation methods.

Some recipes which might ordinarily have been included in this book are to be found in *Simplified Quantity Recipes (Nursing/Convalescent Homes and Hospitals)* published by The National Restaurant Association in 1974 and since it is hoped that both books will be used together, these recipes were not included here.

Cooks should be instructed to follow recipes exactly, use the size pans specified, and be sure ovens register correct temperatures. Most cooks do not realize that 10% to 15% more weight can be lost from a roast which is cooked at 375°F instead of 325°F. It should be stressed that each 4 ounces of roast which is lost because meat is cooked at a higher temperature means that a serving is lost and the food cost will be higher for the remaining servings.

Pans and other equipment used in this book have been kept to the very minimum generally available in most kitchens but it is important that the size pans specified be used in order to produce a standard product.

Choice-grade meat has been used in testing these recipes. Prime meat is generally quite expensive and is often unavailable. It is often too difficult to cook less tender meat, so most buyers agree that choice grade is most satisfactory for most roasts and steaks, and good or choice meats for stews and ground meats.

The fat content of ground meats will vary from about 15% for ground round to a high of over 30%. Generally speaking, lean beef with a fat content of 20% will yield a good beef patty without too much cooking loss. It is important to specify the fat content of ground beef when it is purchased, since beef with too much fat in it will have too great a cooking loss and beef without enough fat in it will yield a dry, unappetizing product. Most of the ground beef in these recipes is cooked and the fat is drained off and discarded—since most Americans these days are aware of the number of calories in fat and the danger to persons with a tendency toward heart trouble, and they appreciate foods with a lower fat content.

The storage of fresh and cooked meat is as important as the storage of frozen meat. The following principles should be used in the storage of meat:

1. Fresh meat should be stored in the coldest part of the refrigerator. The temperature should be as low as possible without freezing the meat (about 38°F).

2. Prepackaged fresh meat may be stored in the refrigerator in the original wrapping for not over 2 days. It may be stored in the freezer without rewrapping for 1 to 2 weeks. It must be rewrapped in special freezer paper if it is to be stored longer than 1 or 2 weeks.

3. Fresh meat which was not prepackaged should be removed from the wrapping paper and wrapped loosely in wax paper or aluminum foil. It may be refrigerated for up to 2 days.

4. Variety meats and ground or chopped meats are more perishable than other meats and should be cooked in 1 or 2 days if not frozen.

5. Cured, or cured and smoked, meats and sausage should be stored in the refrigerator. They should be left in their original wrappings. Canned hams and other perishable canned meats should be stored in the refrigerator unless storage recommendations on the can state otherwise. These meats should not be frozen.

6. Frozen meat should be put in the freezer as soon as it is delivered unless it is to be defrosted for cooking. It is a good idea to date the packages as they are put into the freezer as a record of their age and guide for their use. Storage time should be limited in order to serve them at their prime. The temperature of the freezer should be kept at 0°F or colder.

7. Leftover meats should be cooled as rapidly as possible, then covered or wrapped and stored in the refrigerator. Most dishes prepared in pots may be put in a sink surrounded by cold water. However, pans which cannot be cooled that way should be put warm into the refrigerator. Roasts which are not to be carved immediately should be allowed to set for about 15 to 20 minutes and then refrigerated.

8. Leftover meat should be left in as big pieces as possible to prevent bacterial contamination. Bones may be removed to save space but meat should not be ground, chopped, or sliced until it is to be used.

9. Frozen meat may be defrosted before it is cooked or it may be cooked from the frozen state. However, it is important to allow additional cooking time for meat cooked from the frozen state. Frozen roasts require an additional 30% to 50% cooking time depending upon the thickness of the roast. Additional cooking time for roasts and chops will vary according to the thickness of the meat. It is not advisable to cook and stir ground beef from the frozen state, since it is impossible to cook the meat evenly when it is frozen in bulk but it is acceptable to cook patties and salisbury steaks or meat loaves which have previously been shaped and frozen.

10. The most desirable way to defrost frozen meat is in the refrigerator. The meat should be defrosted in the wrappings. Defrosting in water is not recommended unless the meat is to be cooked in the liquid. After meat is defrosted, it should be cooked the same as fresh meat.

11. It is not desirable to refreeze meat which has been defrosted because of the danger of bacterial contamination while it was being defrosted.

BEEF PASTIES
(Northern Michigan)

YIELD: 50 portions
PAN SIZE: 18 × 26-inch sheet pans
PORTION SIZE: 1 pastie
TEMPERATURE: 400°F Oven

INGREDIENTS	WEIGHTS/MEASURES	FOR _____	METHOD
Sifted all-purpose flour Shortening	1¾ gallons (7 pounds) 2¼ quarts (4 pounds)		1. Sift flour into mixer bowl. Add shortening. Mix on low speed about ½ minute or until mixture resembles coarse meal. OR Cut shortening into flour with a pastry knife until mixture resembles coarse meal.
Cold water (40° to 50°F) Salt	1½ quarts ⅓ cup		2. Dissolve salt in water. Add to flour mixture. Mix at low speed about 1 minute or until dough is just formed. 3. Divide dough into fifty 4½-ounce balls. Cover and refrigerate at least 1 hour.
Round steak, trimmed and cut into ½-inch cubes White potatoes, peeled and cut into ½-inch cubes Carrots, cleaned and cut into ½-inch cubes Chopped onions Salt Pepper Canned condensed cream of mushroom soup	8 pounds 6 ounces 1½ gallons 2 quarts 2 quarts 3 tablespoons 1½ teaspoons 1 quart		4. Combine meat, potatoes, carrots, and onions. Mix lightly to distribute meat throughout potatoes and vegetables. Add salt, pepper, and soup and mix lightly. 5. Roll each piece of dough about ⅛-inch thick on a lightly floured board to form 9-inch rounds. 6. Put 1 cup filling in the center of each circle. Fold one side of the pastry circle half way over the filling. Turn the other side up to meet the first and press the dough together across the top. Crimp the sides together and fold over to seal the pastry. The pastie should be about 9 inches long and 4 inches across with a decorative edge along the center where the pastry has been crimped together. 7. Transfer each pastie to an ungreased sheet pan with a spatula. The sides of the pasties should

(continued)

INGREDIENTS	WEIGHTS/MEASURES	FOR _____	METHOD
			not touch each other. DO NOT CUT VENTS IN THE PASTRY. 8. Bake 45 minutes to 1 hour or until pastie is browned. Serve hot. Pasties may also be served at room temperature for picnics.

DIETARY INFORMATION:

May be used as written for general diets.
This recipe provides 2 ounces protein per portion.

BOILED DINNER
(New England)

YIELD: 50 portions
PAN SIZE: Heavy 5-gallon stockpot
PORTION SIZE: 3 ounces corned beef and $1\frac{1}{2}$ cups vegetables
TEMPERATURE:

INGREDIENTS	WEIGHTS/MEASURES	FOR ___	METHOD
Fresh corned beef Cold water	17 pounds As necessary		1. Place whole pieces of corned beef in stockpot. Cover with water. Bring to a boil. Cover and simmer about 5 hours or until tender. (Smaller pieces will be tender first.) Remove scum as it rises to the surface during the cooking period. 2. Remove tender corned beef from liquid. 3. Remove any excess fat from top of liquid. Pour liquid into a roasting pan or other pan with a larger top surface which can be used for cooking vegetables.
Quartered fresh carrots Quartered rutabagas Quartered medium-size onions	1 gallon (about 5 pounds) 1 gallon (about 5 pounds) 2 quarts (about 2 pounds 8 ounces)		4. Bring cooking liquid to a boil. Add carrots, rutabagas, and onions. Cook 10 minutes.
Quartered fresh white potatoes	12 pounds (about $2\frac{3}{4}$ gallons)		5. Add potatoes to vegetables. Return to a boil and continue to cook another 10 minutes.
Fresh cabbage wedges	50 (about 15 pounds)		6. Place cabbage wedges on top of vegetables in broth and continue to cook another 15 minutes. 7. Serve vegetables hot with thin slices of corned beef.

(continued)

DIETARY INFORMATION:

May be used as written for general, bland, and high-fiber diets.

Diabetic: This recipe provides 3 meat and 1½ bread exchanges per portion.

This recipe provides 3 ounces protein per portion.

NOTES:

1. A bowl of the cooking liquid may be served to use on the vegetables.
2. Vegetables may be cooked or steamed separately if desired, although it is customary to cook them in one pot.

CHILI
(Chicago)

YIELD: 50 portions (about 3 gallons)
PAN SIZE: Heavy 5-gallon stockpot
PORTION SIZE: 1 cup (8 ounces)
TEMPERATURE:

INGREDIENTS	WEIGHTS/MEASURES	FOR _____	METHOD
Chopped onions Vegetable oil Lean ground beef	1 quart ¼ cup 8 pounds		1. Fry onions in oil in stockpot over low heat, stirring occasionally, until onions are golden. Add beef and cook and stir over medium heat until meat is broken up and well browned. Pour meat into colander and drain off fat and liquid. Discard fat and liquid and return meat and onions to stockpot.
Crushed solid-pack canned tomatoes Tomato sauce Salt Pepper Paprika Sugar Chili powder Garlic powder Ground oregano Cumin Hot fat-free chicken broth	3 quarts (1 No. 10 can) 3 quarts (1 No. 10 can) 3 tablespoons 2 teaspoons 2 tablespoons 2 tablespoons 2 tablespoons 2 teaspoons 2 teaspoons 1 teaspoon 2½ quarts		2. Add tomatoes, tomato sauce, salt, pepper, paprika, sugar, chili powder, garlic powder, oregano, cumin, and chicken broth to meat. Simmer uncovered for 1 hour and 15 minutes. Skim any fat off of chili.
Drained cooked kidney or pinto beans	3 quarts		3. Add beans to chili. Simmer 15 minutes and serve hot.

(continued)

DIETARY INFORMATION:

May be used as written for general, high-fiber and low-cholesterol diets.

Diabetic: This recipe provides $1\frac{1}{2}$ bread and 3 meat exchanges per portion.

This recipe provides 2 ounces protein per portion.

NOTES: This is a mild chili. If a hotter chili is desired, add 1 teaspoon ground red pepper in step 2 and use as much chili powder as desired.

Variations:
1. *CHILI-MAC:* Cook 2 pounds 8 ounces ($2\frac{1}{2}$ quarts) elbow macaroni. Drain well and add to chili just before serving.
2. *CHILI WITH RICE:* Cook 2 pounds 12 ounces ($1\frac{1}{2}$ quarts) long-grain rice. Put $\frac{1}{2}$ cup cooked rice in a bowl. Cover with 1 cup chili and serve hot.

CHILI
(Texas)

YIELD: 50 portions (about 3 gallons)
PAN SIZE: Heavy 5-gallon stockpot
PORTION SIZE: 1 cup (8 ounces)
TEMPERATURE:

INGREDIENTS	WEIGHTS/MEASURES	FOR ___	METHOD
Dried pinto beans Water Salt Bacon fat	2 pounds 8 ounces ($5\frac{1}{2}$ to 6 cups) 1 gallon 2 tablespoons 3 tablespoons		1. Wash beans thoroughly and place in stockpot. Add 1 gallon water. Bring to a boil and cook 2 minutes. Remove from heat and let stand, covered, for 1 hour. Drain well. 2. Cover beans with water. Add salt and bacon fat. Cover and simmer 1 hour or until tender. Add water, if necessary, to keep the beans covered with water while they are cooking.
Vegetable oil Chili meat	2 tablespoons 12 pounds		3. Heat oil in stockpot. Add meat ($\frac{1}{2}$- to $\frac{3}{4}$-inch ground beef, or beef chuck which has been boned and cut into $\frac{3}{4}$-inch cubes) and cook over medium heat, stirring frequently, until pink color is gone.
Minced garlic cloves OR Garlic powder Chili powder Salt Ground cumin Hot water	8 1 tablespoon $\frac{3}{4}$ to 1 cup 3 tablespoons 2 tablespoons $1\frac{1}{2}$ gallons		4. Add garlic, chili powder, salt, and cumin to meat. Cook and stir over medium heat about 5 minutes or until meat is coated with the seasonings. 5. Add water to meat. Bring to a boil. Reduce heat, cover and simmer for 1 hour, stirring occasionally.
Corn meal or masa Water	$1\frac{1}{3}$ cups 1 cup		6. Mix cornmeal or masa and water together and stir into chili mixture. Simmer, uncovered, for 30 minutes, stirring frequently to prevent sticking. 7. Add beans and juice to chili. Reheat to boiling, stirring to prevent sticking.
Chopped onions Saltine crackers	1 quart 2 pounds		8. Serve chili in a bowl topped with a heaping tablespoon of chopped onions accompanied by crackers.

(continued)

DIETARY INFORMATION:

May be used as written for general and high-fiber diets.

Diabetic: This recipe provides 3 meat, 2 bread, and 1 fat exchanges per portion.

This recipe provides 3 ounces protein per portion.

NOTES:

1. This recipe was provided by Frances Lee, a consulting dietition from Kerens, Texas. Mrs. Lee adds that Texans have many different versions of this recipe which lead to many chili cook-offs. Coarsely ground beef is generally simmered until tender and then a special blend of seasoning is added. The mixture is usually thickened with masa (corn flour), corn meal, flour, oatmeal, or instant potatoes. Tomatoes are not generally added in that section of Texas.
2. The chili powder can be cut to $\frac{1}{4}$ cup in step 4 if a milder chili is desired.
3. One and one-third No. 10 cans of canned pinto beans may be used instead of dried beans. Add in step 7 instead of the cooked dried beans.

HOT SPICED CORNED BEEF SANDWICHES
(Midwestern)

YIELD: 50 portions (about 3¼ quarts)
PAN SIZE: 10 × 12 × 2-inch steam table pan
PORTION SIZE: 1 sandwich
TEMPERATURE: 350°F Oven

INGREDIENTS	WEIGHTS/MEASURES	FOR ___	METHOD
Canned corned beef Salad dressing Catsup Horseradish mustard	4 pounds 1 quart 2 cups 1 cup		1. Put corned beef in mixer bowl and mix at low speed for ½ minute or until corned beef is broken up. Add salad dressing, catsup and mustard. Mix only until slightly chunky, not smooth. Spread evenly in a half steam table pan and bake, uncovered, for 20 to 25 minutes.
Hamburger buns	50		2. Serve ¼ cup (No. 16 dipper) on each bun which has been toasted or warmed on the grill.

DIETARY INFORMATION:
May be used as written for general diets.
Each sandwich provides 1 ounce protein.

NOTES: This recipe was furnished by Hazel Sorensen of Kennedy's Super-Valu restaurant, Oelwein, Iowa.

CREOLE MACARONI
(Southern)

YIELD: 50 portions (3 pans)　　　　　　　　　　　　　　　　**PORTION SIZE:** 1 cup
PAN SIZE: Heavy 3-gallon stockpot　　　　　　　　　　　　　**TEMPERATURE:** 350°F Oven
　　　　　　　12 × 20 × 2-inch steam table pans

INGREDIENTS	WEIGHTS/MEASURES	FOR ____	METHOD
Elbow macaroni Boiling water Salt Vegetable oil	2 pounds 8 ounces (2½ quarts) 1½ gallons 4 tablespoons 2 tablespoons		1. Combine macaroni, water, salt, and oil in stockpot. Cook and stir until boiling. Boil, stirring frequently, for 2 minutes. Remove from heat, cover and let stand until needed for step 4. (Macaroni should stand about 30 to 40 minutes.) Drain well.
Chopped onions Chopped fresh green peppers Minced garlic Shortening	2 cups 2¼ cups 3 cloves ½ cup		2. Fry onions, green peppers, and garlic in shortening over medium heat, stirring frequently, until onions are tender.
All-purpose flour Tomato paste Canned crushed tomatoes Hot water Salt Pepper Hot sauce	1 cup 1½ quarts (one-half No. 10 can) 1½ quarts (one-half No. 10 can) 3 quarts ⅓ cup 1 tablespoon 1½ teaspoons		3. Sprinkle flour over vegetables. Add tomato paste, tomatoes, water, salt, pepper, sugar, and hot sauce. Stir to blend well. Simmer 10 to 15 minutes over low heat, stirring occasionally. Set aside for use in step 4.
Lean ground beef	5 pounds		4. Brown beef in heavy frying pan over medium heat, stirring frequently, until well browned. Drain well to remove fat and liquids. Discard fat and liquid and combine browned beef with cooked drained macaroni and tomato sauce. Pour one-third of the mixture (about 1 gallon) into each of 3 steam table pans.
			(continued)

INGREDIENTS	WEIGHTS/MEASURES	FOR _____	METHOD
Shredded cheddar cheese	3 cups (12 ounces)		5. Sprinkle 1 cup cheese evenly over the mixture in each pan. 6. Bake 20 to 30 minutes or until mixture is bubbling and the cheese is melted.

DIETARY INFORMATION:

May be used as written for general diets.
Diabetic: This recipe provides 1½ meat, 1½ bread, and 1½ fat exchanges per portion.
This recipe provides 1½ ounces protein per portion.

NOTES: Other shapes of macaroni may be substituted for the elbow macaroni in step 1.

ENCHILADAS
(Southwestern)

YIELD: 50 portions (2 pans)
PAN SIZE: 18 × 26-inch sheet pans

PORTION SIZE: 2 enchiladas
TEMPERATURE: 350°F hot fat
350°F Grill

INGREDIENTS	WEIGHTS/MEASURES	FOR ____	METHOD
SAUCE: Minced garlic cloves Shortening All-purpose flour Salt Chili powder Red pepper Hot water Tomato paste	3 2 cups 3 cups 2 tablespoons ¾ cup 1 teaspoon 5½ quarts 1¾ cups		1. Fry garlic in shortening in stockpot. Mix flour, salt, chili powder, and pepper together. Add to garlic and shortening. Cook and stir over low heat until smooth to form a roux. 2. Mix water and tomato paste. Bring to a boil and add all at once to roux. Cook and stir using a wire whip over medium heat until smooth. Simmer, stirring occasionally about 15 minutes. Set aside for later use.
FILLING: Lean ground beef Minced garlic cloves All-purpose flour Chili powder Red pepper Salt	9 pounds 3 ¼ cup ¾ cup 1 teaspoon 1½ tablespoons		1. Cook and stir meat over moderate heat until it is broken up and has lost its pink color. Drain well. Discard fat and liquid and return to stockpot. Add garlic. 2. Mix flour, chili powder, pepper, and salt. Sprinkle over meat and mix well. Add 2½ quarts sauce. Mix well. Simmer, uncovered, for 30 minutes, stirring occasionally. Set aside for later use.
PANNING INSTRUCTIONS: Tortillas Filling Chopped onions Shredded cheese Sauce	100 5 quarts 2½ quarts 3 pounds (2¼ quarts) 3½ quarts		1. Prepare tortillas, not more than 12 at a time. Fry each tortilla about 15 seconds in hot fat or heat about 30 seconds on grill, turning frequently. Stack tortillas to keep them warm. Fill immediately and roll. It is best to have two people working at this to keep the tortillas from getting cold.

(continued)

INGREDIENTS	WEIGHTS/MEASURES	FOR _____	METHOD
			2. Place 2 tablespoons meat filling, 1½ tablespoons onions and 1 tablespoon shredded cheese in the center of each tortilla. Roll tortilla tightly around filling. Keep remaining onions and cheese for topping. 3. Spread 2 cups sauce in the bottom of each sheet pan, just enough for a very thin layer. 4. Line up 50 tortillas on each pan placing them side by side, seam down, with edges touching. 5. Pour 1¼ quarts sauce evenly over the enchiladas in each pan. Bake 15 minutes or only until thoroughly heated. 6. Sprinkle remaining onions and cheese over each pan just before serving. Serve hot.

DIETARY INFORMATION:

May be used as written for general diets for those accustomed to highly spiced foods.

Diabetic: This recipe provides 2½ bread, 3 meat, and 4 fat (plus fat in meat) exchanges per portion.

This recipe provides 3 ounces protein per portion.

NOTES:

1. This is a rather hot sauce. If a milder sauce is desired, delete red pepper and cut chili powder to ⅓ cup in step 1 in sauce and step 2 in filling.
2. Other fillings may also be used for enchiladas using the same sauce and topping.

MARTHA'S COMPANY CASSEROLE

YIELD: 50 portions (2 pans)
PAN SIZE: Heavy 3- and 5-gallon stockpots
12 × 20 × 2-inch steam table pans

PORTION SIZE: 1 cup (8 ounces)
TEMPERATURE: 350°F Oven

INGREDIENTS	WEIGHTS/MEASURES	FOR___	METHOD
Lean ground beef	8 pounds 12 ounces		1. Brown meat over moderate heat in stockpot, stirring frequently. Drain well. Discard fat and liquid and return beef to stockpot.
Tomato sauce Salt	3¾ quarts (1¼ No. 10 cans) 3 tablespoons		2. Add tomato sauce and salt to beef. Cover and simmer 10 minutes.
Egg noodles Hot water Salt Vegetable oil	4 pounds 4 gallons ¼ cup 2 tablespoons		3. Stir noodles into boiling salted water. Add oil. Cook about 10 to 12 minutes or until noodles are barely tender. Drain well.
Cottage cheese Cream cheese Sour cream Chopped green onions and tops Chopped fresh green peppers	5 pounds 4 pounds 2 cups 3 cups ½ cup		4. Combine cottage cheese, cream cheese, and sour cream. Mix until smooth. Add onions and peppers and mix lightly. 5. Put one-quarter of the noodles (about 2½ quarts) in the bottom of each of 2 steam table pans. Spread one-half of the cheese mixture evenly over the noodles in each pan. Spread one-half of the remaining noodles over the cheese in each pan. Cover noodles using one-half of the meat sauce for each pan. 6. Bake 1 hour. Serve hot.

DIETARY INFORMATION:

May be used as written for general diets. This recipe provides about 3 ounces protein per portion.

NOTES: This casserole may be prepared a few hours ahead of time and refrigerated until needed. If casserole is refrigerated, baking time should be increased to 1½ hours.

MEAT LOAF

YIELD: 50 portions (4 loaves)
PAN SIZE: 18 × 26-inch sheet pan

PORTION SIZE: 4½ ounces
TEMPERATURE: 350°F Oven

INGREDIENTS	WEIGHTS/MEASURES	FOR _____	METHOD
Eggs Nonfat dry milk Very hot water	1¼ quarts (25 medium) 1½ cups 1 quart		1. Whip eggs at moderate speed in mixer bowl for ½ minute. 2. Stir milk into very hot water. Water should be almost but not quite boiling. Pour hot milk into eggs, beating constantly at moderate speed. Stop mixer. Remove whip and substitute beater for the remaining mixing.
Lean ground beef Lean ground pork Tomato juice Salt Pepper Chopped onions Dry bread crumbs	9 pounds 2 pounds 2 cups ¼ cup ½ teaspoon 2 cups 2 quarts (2 pounds)		3. Add beef, pork, tomato juice, salt, pepper, chopped onions and bread crumbs to egg mixture. Mix 2 or 3 minutes at low speed or only until combined. Do not overmix. 4. Remove mixture from mixer. Shape into 4 equal loaves. Place loaves on lightly greased sheet pan and bake 1½ to 1¾ hours or until browned and firm. 5. Let loaves set 10 to 15 minutes and then slice into 4½-ounce portions, 12 to 13 per loaf.

DIETARY INFORMATION:

May be used as written for general diets.
Diabetic: This recipe provides 3 meat and 1 bread exchanges per portion.
This recipe provides 3 ounces protein per portion.

ARGO MEAT LOAF

YIELD: 50 portions (4 loaves)　　　　　　　　　　**PORTION SIZE:** 1 slice (4 ounces)
PAN SIZE: 18 × 26-inch sheet pan　　　　　　　　**TEMPERATURE:** 350°F Oven

INGREDIENTS	WEIGHTS/MEASURES	FOR ___	METHOD
Lean ground beef	8 pounds		1. Put beef, pork, eggs, crumbs, onions, green peppers, salt, sugar, horseradish, catsup, and milk in mixer bowl. Mix at low speed 2 minutes or until blended. Do not overmix.
Lean ground pork	4 pounds		
Eggs	8		
Fine cracker crumbs	1½ quarts		
Chopped onions	½ cup		2. Remove mixture from mixer. Shape into 4 equal loaves, about 4 pounds each.
Chopped fresh green peppers	½ cup		3. Put loaves on lightly greased sheet pan. Bake 1¾ hours or until browned and firm. Dip off any fat which accumulates in the pan.
Salt	2 tablespoons		
Sugar	2 tablespoons		
Horseradish	½ cup		4. Let loaves set 10 to 15 minutes and then slice into 4-ounce portions (12 to 13 slices per loaf).
Catsup	½ cup		
Milk	1 quart		

DIETARY INFORMATION:

May be used as written for general diets.
Diabetic: This recipe provides 3 meat and ½ bread exchanges per portion.
May be used for mild 2- to 3-gram sodium-restricted diets if water is used instead of milk.
This recipe provides 3 ounces protein per portion.

NOTES: This recipe was furnished by Bonnie Lee, head of the Home Economics Department at Argo High School, Argo, Illinois, where it is used in the large-quantity foods preparation class.

Variation:
MEAT LOAF (Midwestern): Delete sugar, horseradish, catsup, and fresh green peppers in basic recipe. Add 1 tablespoon poultry seasoning. Increase chopped onions to 1 quart and bake as directed in basic recipe.

REUBEN SANDWICHES

YIELD: 50 sandwiches
PAN SIZE:

PORTION SIZE: 1 sandwich
TEMPERATURE: 375°F Grill
　　　　　　　　　450°F Oven

INGREDIENTS	WEIGHTS/MEASURES	FOR ____	METHOD
Cooked corned beef	6 pounds 4 ounces		1. Slice corned beef into thin slices about 19 to 25 to the pound.
Rye bread Thousand Island dressing Drained sauerkraut Sliced Swiss cheese Melted margarine	6 pounds (100 slices) 1 quart 1½ quarts 3 pounds 2 ounces (fifty 1-ounce slices) 2 cups (1 pound)		2. Spread each slice of bread with dressing. 3. Place 2 ounces (3 to 4 slices) corned beef on dressing on 1 slice bread. Top with 2 tablespoons sauerkraut and 1 slice cheese. Top with another slice of bread with dressing on cheese. 4. Brush the outside of each sandwich with melted margarine and grill until lightly browned on both sides or arrange sandwiches on sheet pans and bake for 10 minutes or until lightly browned. Serve hot.

DIETARY INFORMATION:

May be used as written for general and high-fiber diets.
Each sandwich provides 3 ounces protein.

ROAST BEEF HASH

YIELD: 50 portions (3 pans)
PAN SIZE: 12 × 20 × 2-inch steam table pans
PORTION SIZE: 1 cup
TEMPERATURE: 350°F Oven

INGREDIENTS	WEIGHTS/MEASURES	FOR_____	METHOD
Cooked beef	9 pounds 6 ounces (about 1¾ gallons)		1. Cut beef which has been trimmed with fat and gristle removed into about ½-inch cubes. (The quality of the finished hash will depend upon the quality of the beef used.)
Chopped onions Chopped fresh green peppers Minced garlic cloves Shortening	2¼ quarts 2¼ quarts 5 1 cup		2. Fry onions, green peppers, and garlic in frying pan over medium heat, stirring frequently, until onions are golden. Remove vegetables from pan with a slotted spoon and add to beef. Mix well.
Cooked peeled diced white potatoes Pepper Salt Monosodium glutamate	12 pounds (about 2¼ gallons) 2 teaspoons 3 tablespoons 1 tablespoon		3. Carefully mix potatoes, pepper, salt, and monosodium glutamate with beef mixture. Place one-third of the mixture in each of 3 well-buttered steam table pans. (This will yield a slightly crusty hash. If a softer hash is desired, place one-half of the mixture in each of 2 well-buttered steam table pans.)
Hot beef stock Catsup Worcestershire sauce	2 quarts 2 cups 1 tablespoon		4. Combine beef stock (which has been chilled and had the fat removed) with catsup and Worcestershire sauce. Pour one-third of the mixture (about 3⅓ cups) over the mixture in each pan. 5. Cover pans with aluminum foil and bake for 45 minutes. Remove cover and continue baking for 15 minutes or until lightly browned.

(continued)

DIETARY INFORMATION:

May be used as written for general diets.
Diabetic: This recipe provides 3 meat, 1 bread, and 1 fat exchanges per portion.
Low-cholesterol: Use vegetable oil or margarine in step 2 and use margarine to grease pans in step 3.
This recipe provides 3 ounces protein per portion.

NOTES: 15 pounds fresh white potatoes will yield about 12 pounds peeled and cooked potatoes.

STEAK RANCHERO
(Southwestern)

YIELD: 50 portions (2 pans)
PAN SIZE: 12 × 20 × 2-inch steam table pans
PORTION SIZE: 1 steak plus sauce
TEMPERATURE: 325°F Oven

INGREDIENTS	WEIGHTS/MEASURES	FOR ___	METHOD
All purpose flour Salt Chili powder Paprika Dehydrated garlic	2 cups ¼ cup ¼ cup 2 tablespoons 1 tablespoon		1. Mix flour, salt, chili powder, paprika and garlic together to blend.
Portion-cut steaks Vegetable oil	50 5-ounce steaks (about 15 pounds 12 ounces) As necessary		2. Dredge steaks in seasoned flour and brown in vegetable oil in heavy frying pan over medium heat. Put steaks as they are browned in steam table pans, 25 steaks to each pan.
Chopped fresh green peppers Chopped onions	1 quart 1 quart		3. Fry green peppers and onions in oil in frying pan in which steaks were fried. Remove with a slotted spoon and put one-half of the fried onions and green peppers on top of the meat in each pan. Pour fat out of pan.
Beef broth Condensed tomato soup Chili powder Minced garlic cloves Sugar Ground cumin	1 quart 1½ quarts (1 46-ounce can) 2 tablespoons 4 ½ cup 1 teaspoon		4. Pour broth into frying pan and cook and stir until brown bits in pan are absorbed in broth. Add soup, chili powder, garlic, sugar, and cumin. Bring to a boil. Cook 1 minute and then pour one-half of the hot sauce over steaks in each pan. 5. Cover tightly and bake 1½ hours or until steaks are tender. Serve steaks hot with sauce.

DIETARY INFORMATION:

May be used as written for general diets for those accustomed to highly spiced foods.
Low-cholesterol: May be used for low-cholesterol for those accustomed to highly spiced foods if fat is removed from steaks in step 2.
This recipe provides 4 ounces protein per portion.

TACOS
(Southwestern)

YIELD: 50 portions (100 tacos)
PAN SIZE: 12 × 20 × 2-inch steam table pan
PORTION SIZE: 2 tacos
TEMPERATURE: 350°F hot fat
350°F Grill

INGREDIENTS	WEIGHTS/MEASURES	FOR _____	METHOD
Lean ground beef Minced garlic cloves Salt Red pepper Chili powder Tomato sauce	9 pounds 3 3 tablespoons 1/4 teaspoon 1/4 cup 2 cups		1. Cook and stir meat in stockpot over medium heat until meat is broken up and the pink is gone. Drain well. Discard liquid and fat and return meat to stockpot. Add garlic, salt, pepper, and chili powder. Cook meat over medium heat, stirring frequently, until well browned. Add tomato sauce and continue to cook and stir another 4 or 5 minutes.
Tortillas	100		2. Fry each tortilla 15 seconds in hot fat or heat about 30 seconds on grill, turning frequently. Fold in half to form a shell. 3. Place 2 tablespoons meat filling on each tortilla. Line shells in a steam table pan to keep warm or serve immediately.
Shredded cheddar cheese Finely shredded lettuce Chopped onions Taco sauce	3 pounds (about 2 1/4 quarts) 3 pounds (about 3 quarts) 4 1/2 cups As necessary		4. Serve tacos by putting about 1 1/2 tablespoons cheese on top of meat filling. Top cheese with about 2 tablespoons lettuce. Serve warm with taco sauce for those who want it.

DIETARY INFORMATION:
May be used for general diets for those accustomed to highly spiced foods.
Diabetic: This recipe provides 2 bread and 3 meat exchanges per portion.
This recipe provides 3 ounces protein per portion.

NOTES: Tortillas may be purchased fried and folded, and then heated in a microwave oven just before they are filled. They may also be folded around the filling to form a roll instead of a half-moon shape.

TOSTADOS
(Southwestern)

YIELD: 50 portions (50 tostados)
PAN SIZE:

PORTION SIZE: 1 tostado
TEMPERATURE: 350°F hot fat
350°F Grill

INGREDIENTS	WEIGHTS/MEASURES	FOR _____	METHOD
Hot refried beans	12½ cups (1 No. 10 can)		1. Use warm canned refried beans or prepare beans according to recipe on page 147.
Warm taco filling	12½ cups		2. Use 1 recipe of taco filling prepared according to recipe on page 62.
Guacamole	About 2 quarts		3. Prepare guacamole according to recipe on page 126.
Corn tortillas	50		4. Fry each tortilla about 15 seconds in hot fat or heat about 30 seconds on grill, turning frequently. Place flat tortilla on sandwich plate.
Shredded lettuce	3 pounds (about 3 quarts)		5. Spread tortilla with about ¼ cup (No. 16 dipper) refried beans. Sprinkle with about 2 tablespoons shredded cheese. Spread about ¼ cup (No. 16 dipper) taco filling on cheese. Spread about ½ cup shredded lettuce over filling. Put about 1 tablespoon guacamole in the center of the lettuce.
Shredded mild cheddar cheese	2 pounds (1½ quarts)		6. Serve immediately since the contrast between the hot and cold, crisp and soft is important for a successful tostado.
Hot sauce	As necessary		7. Serve hot sauce for those who want it.

DIETARY INFORMATION:

May be used for general and high-fiber diets for those accustomed to highly spiced foods.
Diabetic: This recipe provides 2 bread, 5 meat, and 7 fat exchanges per portion.
This recipe provides 5 ounces protein per portion.

BROILED LAMB PATTIES

YIELD: 50 portions　　　　　　　　　　　　　　　　　　　　　　**PORTION SIZE:** 1 pattie
PAN SIZE:　　　　　　　　　　　　　　　　　　　　　　　　　　**TEMPERATURE:**

INGREDIENTS	WEIGHTS/MEASURES	FOR ___	METHOD
Ground lamb	14 pounds		1. Place ingredients in mixer bowl in order given. Mix at low speed 1 to 2 minutes or until blended.
Dry bread crumbs	1½ quarts		2. Shape into 4 ounce patties using No. 8 dipper of meat mixture. Handle as lightly as possible. Do not press down on meat to form a too firm pattie.
Finely chopped onions	3 cups		3. Broil patties at medium heat 12 minutes on one side. Turn and broil 10 minutes for well done patties.
Milk	1 cup		4. Serve hot.
Salt	3 tablespoons		
Pepper	1 teaspoon		
Worcestershire sauce	¼ cup		

DIETARY INFORMATION:
May be used as written for general diets.
Diabetic: This recipe provides 3 meat exchanges per portion.
This recipe provides 3 ounces protein per portion.

NOTES: Shelly Lein won first place in an outdoor barbecue contest at a Bicentennial celebration in Fayette County, Iowa, with this recipe for broiled lamb patties.

SIMMERED CHITTERLINGS

YIELD: 50 portions (about 2¼ gallons)
PAN SIZE: Heavy stockpot
PORTION SIZE: ⅔ cup (4 ounces)
TEMPERATURE:

INGREDIENTS	WEIGHTS/MEASURES	FOR _____	METHOD
Frozen chitterlings	38 pounds		1. Cover chitterlings with water to thaw. 2. Wash chitterlings under cool running water. Strip fat particles from lining while washing. Chitterlings must be washed until they are clean and white. Put in stockpot.
Water	As necessary		3. Cover chitterlings with water. Cover and simmer 1½ hours. Drain well.
Vinegar Cool water	2 cups 2 gallons		4. Rinse chitterlings well in vinegar water. Cut into about 6-inch lengths.
Water Salt Sugar Poultry seasoning Red pepper Black pepper	As necessary 1½ tablespoons 1 tablespoon 1 teaspoon 1 teaspoon 1½ tablespoons		5. Return chitterlings to stockpot. Add enough water to cover them. Add salt, sugar, poultry seasoning, red and black pepper. Cover and simmer another 2 hours. 6. Put chitterlings in serving pans. Cover with cooking liquid. Serve hot.

DIETARY INFORMATION:

May be used as written for general diets.

NOTES:

Variation:
DEEP FAT FRIED CHITTERLINGS: Cut pieces into 1- to 1½-inch lengths in step 4. Drain well. Dip in a flour mixture made with 2 quarts cake flour, 2 tablespoons salt and 1½ teaspoons black pepper. Dip in an egg dip made with 2 cups beaten eggs and 2 cups milk. Dip again in flour mixture and fry about 2 minutes or until deep brown in hot (375°F) fat.

HAM LOAF

YIELD: 50 portions (4 loaves)
PAN SIZE: Roaster

PORTION SIZE: 1 slice
TEMPERATURE: 350°F Oven

INGREDIENTS	WEIGHTS/MEASURES	FOR_____	METHOD
Dry bread, broken into pieces Milk	1 pound (about 2½ quarts) 3½ cups		1. Put bread in mixer bowl. Add milk and let stand 5 minutes. Mix at low speed about 1 minute or until smooth.
Chopped onions Eggs Pepper Dry mustard	2 cups 1½ cups (7 to 8 medium) 1 teaspoon 1 tablespoon		2. Add onions, eggs, pepper, and mustard to bread. Mix at low speed for 15 seconds to blend.
Ground cooked ham Lean ground pork	9 pounds 6 pounds		3. Add ham and pork to bread mixture. Mix at low speed 1 minute or until blended. DO NOT OVERMIX. 4. Form meat into 4 equal loaves, about 4 pounds 14 ounces each, and place in roaster. 5. Bake, uncovered, about 1½ to 2 hours or until firm. Spoon out any fat which cooks out into the pan during the cooking period. 6. Cool slightly and cut 13 slices per loaf.

DIETARY INFORMATION:

May be used as written for general diets.
Diabetic: This recipe provides 3 meat and ½ bread exchanges per portion.
This recipe provides 3 ounces protein per portion.

PORK CHOPS IN APRICOT SAUCE
(California)

YIELD: 50 portions
PAN SIZE: 18 × 26-inch sheet pans
Roaster

PORTION SIZE: 1 chop plus sauce
TEMPERATURE: 400° and 350°F Oven

INGREDIENTS	WEIGHTS/MEASURES	FOR ____	METHOD
Pork chops cut 3 to the pound Salt Pepper	50 (about 16 pounds 4 ounces) 2 tablespoons 1/2 teaspoon		1. Arrange chops in a single layer on sheet pans. Sprinkle with salt and pepper. Bake 30 minutes at 400°F or until lightly browned. Pour off any fat. 2. Arrange browned chops in shingle style in roaster. Scrape brown bits from sheet pans and add to chops.
Canned apricot nectar Lemon juice Apricot jam Ground thyme Ground oregano Garlic powder Salt Monosodium glutamate	1 quart 1 cup 1 quart 1 teaspoon 1 teaspoon 1 teaspoon 1 tablespoon 1 teaspoon		3. Combine apricot nectar, lemon juice, apricot jam, thyme, oregano, garlic, salt, and monosodium glutamate. Mix well. Heat to boiling and pour over hot chops in roaster. 4. Cover roaster and bake at 350°F for 30 minutes. Uncover roaster and bake another 30 minutes or until tender and browned, basting frequently.
Hot cooked rice	1 1/2 gallons		5. Serve chops hot over 1/2 cup rice per portion with some of the sauce, or sauce may be mixed with the hot rice and served beside the chop.

DIETARY INFORMATION:

May be used as written for general diets.
This recipe provides 3 ounces protein per portion.

SIMMERED PORK HOCKS

YIELD: 50 portions
PAN SIZE: Heavy 5-gallon stockpot

PORTION SIZE: 1 each
TEMPERATURE:

INGREDIENTS	WEIGHTS/MEASURES	FOR _____	METHOD
Pork hocks	50 10-ounce hocks (about 31 pounds)		1. Place hocks in stockpot. Add water, salt, bay leaves, garlic, red pepper, and onions. Cover and simmer 3 hours or until tender.
Boiling water	3 gallons		
Salt	1/3 cup		
Bay leaves	4		
Garlic	3 cloves		
Red pepper	1 tablespoon		
Coarsely chopped onions	2 cups		

DIETARY INFORMATION:

May be used as written for general diets.
Diabetic: This recipe provides 3 meat exchanges plus fat in meat per portion.
This recipe provides 3 ounces protein per portion.

NOTES:
Variation:
SIMMERED PIGS' FEET: Use 32 pounds of pigs' feet instead of pork hocks. Split pigs' feet in half to serve them.

Chicken

Barbecued Chicken	70
Brunswick Stew (Southern)	71
Chicken and Sauerkraut	73
Chicken-Sausage Gumbo (Acadiana-Cajun)	74
Chicken Spaghetti (Texas)	76
Chicken Vega	77
Country Style Chicken (Maryland)	78
Dirty Rice (Acadiana-Cajun)	79
Escalloped Chicken and Dressing (Midwestern)	81
Fried Chicken (Southern)	83
Giblet Jambalaya (Acadiana-Cajun)	85

Information

Chicken has until recently been very expensive in most countries except our own, and many countries have developed special holiday recipes for chicken. Some of these are not practical for general use but many are used and enjoyed here also. Many regions of the country also have special recipes for chicken and turkey; some of these were included in our first book *Simplified Quantity Recipes (Nursing/Convalescent Homes and Hospitals)*, published in 1974 by the National Restaurant Association, and others are included here.

Our modern chickens are a far cry from the chickens used formerly in our country and abroad. They are younger, meatier, and more tender. They are available in many cuts now, and the recipes in this book have specified the cuts used for each recipe to simplify ordering and preparation of the recipe. They are available fresh, quick frozen, or deep chilled. They are available whole, split, quartered, or in parts. However, it is important to remember that all poultry is highly perishable and extreme care should be taken to keep it clean and pure at all times.

Chicken should never be refrozen once it has been defrosted. However, if there is any leftover cooked chicken, it should be well wrapped in freezer paper or aluminum foil for use in casseroles or other dishes. It should be left in as large chunks as possible and not cut or ground until it is to be used, to help prevent bacterial contamination. It should be labeled, frozen at 0°F, and used within a month.

Fresh chicken should be used whenever possible but if frozen chicken is to be used it should be defrosted in the refrigerator for 24 to 72 hours. Defrosting should be planned so that the chicken can be used as soon as possible after it is defrosted.

Chicken should be washed thoroughly and drained or wiped dry with a clean cloth or paper towel before it is used in most recipes.

BARBECUED CHICKEN

YIELD: 50 portions
PAN SIZE: Heavy 2-gallon stockpot
18 × 26-inch sheet pans

PORTION SIZE: 1/4 chicken (2 pieces)
TEMPERATURE: 325°F Oven

INGREDIENTS	WEIGHTS/MEASURES	FOR _____	METHOD
Finely chopped onions Margarine Vinegar Water Worcestershire sauce Tomato catsup Prepared mustard Brown sugar Salt Pepper	3 cups 1/2 cup (1 stick) 2 cups 1 1/2 quarts 1 cup 1 1/2 quarts 1/3 cup 1 1/2 cups 3 tablespoons 1/2 teaspoon		1. Fry onions in margarine in stockpot over moderate heat, stirring frequently, about 5 minutes or until onions are limp. 2. Add vinegar, water, Worcestershire sauce, catsup, mustard, brown sugar, salt, and pepper to onions. Cook and stir over moderate heat until sauce is boiling. Cover and simmer 10 minutes over low heat.
2 to 2 1/2-pound broiler-fryers cut into 8 pieces	26 to 32 pounds (13 chickens)		3. Wash chicken thoroughly under running cold water. Drain well. Put chicken in container. Pour barbecue sauce over chicken. Cover and refrigerate 2 hours to marinate. Stir sauce and chicken so that each piece of chicken is covered with sauce. Drain well. 4. Place chicken, skin side up, on lightly greased sheet pans. 5. Bake chicken 1 1/2 hours or until tender. Baste chicken with marinade several times during baking. Bake chicken at least 20 minutes after the last basting.

DIETARY INFORMATION:

May be used as written for general diets.
This recipe provides 3 ounces protein per portion.

BRUNSWICK STEW
(Southern)

YIELD: 50 portions (about 3 gallons)
PAN SIZE: Heavy 5-gallon stockpot
PORTION SIZE: 1 cup (8 ounces)
TEMPERATURE:

INGREDIENTS	WEIGHTS/MEASURES	FOR _____	METHOD
Chopped bacon Coarsely chopped onions	1 pound 1½ quarts		1. Fry bacon in stockpot over low heat, stirring frequently, until bacon is crisp. Add onions to bacon and cook, stirring occasionally, until onions are golden.
Chicken broth Drained canned crushed tomatoes and juice Diced raw white potatoes Chopped parsley Salt White pepper	1½ gallons 2 quarts (two-thirds No. 10 can) 3 quarts 2 tablespoons 1 tablespoon 1 teaspoon		2. Add broth, tomatoes, potatoes, parsley, salt, and pepper to stockpot. Cover and simmer 20 minutes.
Diced cooked chicken Diced cooked ham Frozen lima beans Frozen whole-kernel corn Worcestershire sauce Salt	5 pounds 1 pound 8 ounces 5 pounds 5 pounds ⅓ cup As necessary		3. Add chicken, ham, lima beans, corn, and Worcestershire sauce to stew. Cover and cook 20 minutes or until vegetables are tender. Taste for seasoning. Add more salt, if necessary. (The amount of salt needed will depend upon the saltiness of the broth and ham.)
All-purpose flour Cold water	1 cup 2 cups		4. Stir flour into water to form a smooth paste. Pour into hot stew. Cook, stirring occasionally, over moderate heat until smooth and the starchy taste is gone.

(continued)

DIETARY INFORMATION:

May be used as written for general and high-fiber diets.

Low-cholesterol: Delete bacon and fry onions in 1 cup vegetable oil in step 1. Use fat-free broth in step 2. Use 6 pounds 4 ounces chicken which has had all skin and fat removed and delete ham in step 4.

This recipe provides 2 ounces protein per portion.

NOTES: If pre-cooked diced chicken is bought and used, it should be added after step 4. Reheat stew to serving temperature after adding chicken if necessary.

CHICKEN AND SAUERKRAUT

YIELD: 50 portions
PAN SIZE: Roaster
PORTION SIZE: 1/4 chicken (2 pieces) plus vegetables
TEMPERATURE: 350°F Oven

INGREDIENTS	WEIGHTS/MEASURES	FOR ___	METHOD
2- to 2½-pound broiler-fryers	26 to 32 pounds (13 chickens)		1. Wash chicken thoroughly under running cold water. Drain well. Pat chicken dry with a clean cloth or paper towels.
Canned drained sauerkraut Chicken fat or margarine	1½ gallons (2 No. 10 cans) As necessary		2. Spread drained kraut in the bottom of roasting pan which has been well greased with chicken fat or margarine. Arrange chicken pieces over kraut with the boney pieces on the bottom.
Chopped fresh green peppers Chopped onions Chopped celery Hot fat-free chicken broth Soy sauce Pepper	1 quart 1 quart 1 quart 3 quarts 2 cups 1 teaspoon		3. Sprinkle green peppers, onions and celery over chicken. 4. Combine broth, soy sauce, and pepper and pour over chicken and vegetables. 5. Cover roaster tightly and bake 1 hour. Loosen cover and leave it loose on roaster to allow steam to escape and bake another 30 minutes or until chicken is tender. 6. Serve chicken hot with some of the vegetables.

DIETARY INFORMATION:

May be used as written for general and high-fiber diets.
Diabetic: This recipe provides 3 meat, ½ bread, and ½ fat exchanges per portion.
Low-cholesterol: Remove skin and fat from chicken and grease pan with margarine in step 2.
This recipe provides 3 ounces protein per portion.

CHICKEN-SAUSAGE GUMBO
(Acadiana-Cajun)

YIELD: 50 portions (about 3 gallons)
PAN SIZE: Heavy 5-gallon stockpot
PORTION SIZE: 1 cup (8 ounces) plus 1 cup rice
TEMPERATURE: 375°F Oven

INGREDIENTS	WEIGHTS/MEASURES	FOR ___	METHOD
All-purpose flour Vegetable oil	1¾ quarts 3 cups		1. Stir flour and oil together. Place in a shallow pan and brown in the oven, stirring every 15 minutes until mixture (roux) is a dark caramel color.
Water Coarsely ground onions Coarsely ground celery Coarsely ground fresh green peppers	3 gallons plus 1 cup 2 cups 1 cup 1 cup		2. Combine water and coarsely ground onions, celery and green peppers in stockpot. Bring to a boil. Add roux, a small amount at a time, stirring constantly, until all the roux is dissolved.
2½- to 3-pound broiler-fryers cut into 8 pieces Smoked sausage cut into 2-inch links	17 pounds 8 ounces to 21 pounds (7 chickens) 5 pounds		3. Wash chicken thoroughly under running cold water. Drain well. Add with sausage to boiling sauce. Cover and simmer 1 hour.
Salt Cayenne pepper Chopped parsley Chopped green onion tops	5 tablespoons 1 tablespoon 1½ cups 1 cup		4. Add salt and pepper to chicken-sausage mixture. Cover and simmer another hour. 5. Skim any excess fat from gumbo. Add parsley and onion tops. Mix lightly and serve 1 piece chicken with 1 piece sausage and sauce over 1 cup hot cooked rice.
Long-grain rice	3 quarts (5 pounds 8 ounces)		6. Combine rice, water, salt, and oil in a heavy 5-gallon stockpot. Bring to a boil, stirring

(continued)

INGREDIENTS	WEIGHTS/MEASURES	FOR_____	METHOD
Cold water Salt Vegetable oil	1½ gallons ⅓ cup 2 tablespoons		occasionally. Cover tightly and simmer 15 minutes without stirring. If rice is not tender, cover and simmer another 2 or 3 minutes. 7. Uncover rice and allow it to dry and fluff for 3 to 5 minutes. Serve hot with gumbo.

DIETARY INFORMATION:

May be used as written for general diets for patients accustomed to spicy foods.
This recipe provides 3 ounces protein per portion.

NOTES:

1. This recipe was furnished by Pauline Lalande, R.D., of Lafayette, Louisiana. It was tested and standardized at Consolata Home, New Iberia, Louisiana.
2. Gumbo may be baked in a 350°F oven for 2 hours or until chicken is tender, if desired.

CHICKEN SPAGHETTI
(Texas)

YIELD: 50 portions (2¾ gallons)   **PORTION SIZE:** ⅞ cup (7 ounces)
PAN SIZE: Heavy 5-gallon stockpot   **TEMPERATURE:**

INGREDIENTS	WEIGHTS/MEASURES	FOR ____	METHOD
Stewing or frying chickens Water Salt Black pepper Chopped onions Diced celery Diced fresh green peppers	15 pounds 1¾ gallons ¼ cup 1 teaspoon 1 quart 3 cups 2 cups		1. Place chicken in pot. Add water, salt, pepper, onions, celery, and green peppers. Cover and simmer 1 hour or until chicken is tender. 2. Remove chicken from the pot. Cool in the refrigerator. Remove chicken meat from bones. Discard skin and fat and cut chicken into bite-size pieces. Refrigerate chicken for use in step 4.
Cut spaghetti Water	2 pounds 4 ounces As necessary		3. Bring chicken stock and vegetables to a boil. Add spaghetti. Stir. Bring to a boil and cook 10 minutes. Add more water if necessary.
Canned condensed tomato soup Chili powder Grated cheddar cheese (optional)	2 quarts (1⅓ 46-ounce cans) 1 to 2 tablespoons 3 cups (1 pound)		4. Stir soup and chili powder together and add to spaghetti. Stir gently to mix and add chicken. Stir gently to mix. 5. Bring to a simmer and serve hot, garnished with cheese.

DIETARY INFORMATION:

May be used as written for general diets.
Diabetic: This recipe provides 1½ bread and 2 meat exchanges per portion.
This recipe provides 2 ounces protein per portion.

NOTES:

1. This recipe was provided by Frances Lee, a consulting dietitian from Kerens, Texas. Mrs. Lee adds that it is often served for fund-raising dinners accompanied by green beans, cole slaw, and pie.
2. Chicken spaghetti can be placed in a baking pan, sprinkled with cheese, and baked in a 300°F oven for 45 minutes, if desired.

CHICKEN VEGA

YIELD: 50 portions
PAN SIZE: Roaster

PORTION SIZE: 1/4 chicken (2 pieces) plus rice
TEMPERATURE: 375°F Oven

INGREDIENTS	WEIGHTS/MEASURES	FOR _____	METHOD
Long-grain rice Hot water	2½ quarts (about 5 pounds) 3 quarts		1. Put one-half of the rice in each of 2 roasting pans. Pour 1½ quarts of water over rice in each pan and mix.
2- to 2½-pound broiler-fryers cut into 8 pieces	26 to 32 pounds (13 chickens)		2. Wash chicken thoroughly under running cold water. Drain well. Place one-half of the chicken evenly over the rice in each roaster.
Nonfat dry milk Hot water Chicken soup and gravy base	3 cups 1 gallon 1¾ cups		3. Stir dry milk into hot water. Add gravy base and mix well.
Melted butter or margarine Cake flour	1½ cups (3 sticks) 2 cups		4. Stir melted fat and flour together until smooth. Stir into milk mixture. Cook and stir over moderate heat until thickened. Pour one-half of the sauce over the chicken in each roaster.
Dry onion soup mix	2 cups		5. Pour 1 cup of the soup mix evenly over the chicken in each pan. Cover and bake 1 hour and 15 minutes. Remove cover and bake another 30 minutes or until chicken is tender.

DIETARY INFORMATION:

May be used as written for general diets.
Low-cholesterol: Remove skin and fat from chicken in step 2. Use margarine in step 4.
This recipe provides 3 ounces protein per portion.

COUNTRY STYLE CHICKEN
(Maryland)

YIELD: 50 portions
PAN SIZE: Roaster

PORTION SIZE: ¼ chicken (2 pieces)
TEMPERATURE: 325°F Oven

INGREDIENTS	WEIGHTS/MEASURES	FOR _____	METHOD
2- to 2½-pound broiler-fryers cut into 8 pieces	26 to 32 pounds (13 chickens)		1. Wash chicken thoroughly under running cold water. Drain well.
All-purpose flour Salt Pepper Paprika	1¾ quarts ⅓ cup 1½ teaspoons 1 tablespoon		2. Combine flour, salt, pepper, and paprika. Dredge chicken in flour mixture. Shake off excess flour.
Shortening Hot water	2 cups 1 quart		3. Brown chicken in batches in heavy frying pan over moderate heat in shortening. Place chicken pieces in the roaster as they are browned. 4. Pour hot water over chicken. Cover tightly and bake 1 hour or until chicken is tender. 5. Remove chicken from roaster. Keep warm. Put roaster on top of range.
Milk	1 gallon		6. Stir milk into drippings in roaster. Cook and stir over low heat until simmering.
Melted shortening All-purpose flour	1 cup 2 cups		7. Stir shortening and flour together until smooth. Stir into milk mixture. Cook and stir over moderate heat until smooth and thickened and the starchy taste is gone. 8. Serve hot chicken with hot gravy.

DIETARY INFORMATION:

May be used as written for general and mild 2- to 3-gram sodium-restricted diets.

Low-cholesterol: Remove skin and fat from chicken in step 1. Brown chicken in vegetable oil instead of shortening in step 3. Substitute melted margarine for shortening in step 7.

This recipe provides 3 ounces protein per portion.

DIRTY RICE
(Acadiana–Cajun)

YIELD: 50 portions (about 3 gallons)
PAN SIZE: Heavy 5-gallon stockpot
PORTION SIZE: 1 cup (8 ounces)
TEMPERATURE:

INGREDIENTS	WEIGHTS/MEASURES	FOR _____	METHOD
Chicken gizzards	5 pounds		1. Cover gizzards with water. Simmer about 1 hour or until tender. Drain and cool. Trim gristle and fat from gizzards. Chop gizzards and save for use in step 5.
Melted bacon fat All-purpose flour	1 cup 1½ cups		2. Stir flour into melted bacon fat. Cook in heavy frying pan over low heat, stirring frequently, about 15 minutes to make a rich golden brown roux. Save for use in step 5.
Chopped onions Chopped celery Chopped fresh green peppers Vegetable oil	2 quarts 1 quart 1 quart ½ cup		3. Fry onions, celery, and green peppers in vegetable oil in heavy frying pan over moderate heat, stirring frequently, about 10 minutes or until onions are golden. Remove from frying pan with a slotted spoon and set aside for use in step 5.
Lean ground beef	5 pounds		4. Place ground beef in frying pan used to fry vegetables. Cook and stir over moderate heat about 15 minutes until meat is browned and broken up. Drain off all visible fat. Put meat in stockpot.
Hot beef broth Worcestershire sauce Garlic powder Salt Black pepper Red pepper	As necessary (3 to 4 quarts 1 tablespoon 1 teaspoon 1 tablespoon 1 teaspoon 1 teaspoon		5. Add roux and enough beef broth to form a good rich gravy to meat. Cook and stir over moderate heat until smooth. Add vegetables and gizzards. Cook, stirring frequently, for 10 minutes over low heat. The consistency of the mixture should be that of a thick gravy. If it gets too thick a little hot broth may be added.

(continued)

INGREDIENTS	WEIGHTS/MEASURES	FOR _____	METHOD
Long-grain rice	1½ quarts (2 pounds 12 ounces)		6. Combine rice, water, salt, and oil in a heavy 3-gallon stockpot. Bring to a boil, stirring occasionally. Cover tightly and simmer 15 minutes without stirring. If rice is not tender, cover and simmer 2 to 3 minutes longer. 7. Uncover rice and allow it to dry and fluff for 3 to 5 minutes. Toss rice with meat and gravy mixture. Serve hot.
Cold water	3 quarts		
Salt	3 tablespoons		
Vegetable oil	2 tablespoons		

DIETARY INFORMATION:

May be used as written for general and high-fiber diets.
This recipe provides 2 ounces protein per portion.

ESCALLOPED CHICKEN AND DRESSING
(Midwestern)

YIELD: 48 portions (2 pans)
PAN SIZE: 12 × 20 × 2-inch steam table pans
PORTION SIZE: 1 square
TEMPERATURE: 375°F Oven

INGREDIENTS	WEIGHTS/MEASURES	FOR_____	METHOD
Chopped onions Chopped celery Chicken fat or margarine	2¼ cups 3 cups 1½ cups		1. Fry onions and celery in fat in heavy frying pan over medium heat, stirring frequently, until onions are limp.
Eggs Pepper Ground sage Lukewarm fat-free chicken broth Salt	1 cup (5 medium) ¾ teaspoon 1 tablespoon 2¼ quarts As necessary		2. Add onion mixture and fat, eggs, pepper, and sage to chicken broth. Mix to blend. Taste for seasoning and add salt if necessary. The amount of salt necessary will depend upon the saltiness of the broth.
Diced day-old white bread	4 pounds (about 2½ gallons)		3. Place bread cubes in large bowl. Add broth mixture and toss lightly but thoroughly. Spread one-half of the dressing evenly on the bottom of each of 2 buttered steam table pans.
All-purpose flour Melted chicken fat or margarine Hot fat-free chicken broth Salt	2 cups 2 cups 1 gallon As necessary		4. Stir flour and melted fat together to blend. Add to hot broth and cook and stir over medium heat until smooth. Taste for seasoning and add salt, if necessary.
Diced cooked chicken with fat and skin removed	6 pounds		5. Stir chicken into hot sauce. Spoon one-half of the sauce evenly over the dressing in each pan.
Cornflake crumbs Paprika	2 cups 2 tablespoons		6. Mix crumbs and paprika and spread one-half of the mixture evenly over the top of the chicken and

(continued)

INGREDIENTS	WEIGHTS/MEASURES	FOR _____	METHOD
			sauce in each pan. Do not mix the crumbs into the sauce. 7. Bake 45 minutes to 1 hour or until top is golden and dressing is baked. 8. Cut each pan 4 × 6 and serve hot.

DIETARY INFORMATION:

May be used as written for general diets.

FRIED CHICKEN
(Southern)

YIELD: 50 portions
PAN SIZE: Heavy frying pan
PORTION SIZE: ¼ chicken (2 pieces)
TEMPERATURE:

INGREDIENTS	WEIGHTS/MEASURES	FOR _____	METHOD
2- to 2½-pound broiler-fryers cut into 8 pieces Salt	26 to 32 pounds (13 chickens) 3 tablespoons		1. Wash chickens thoroughly under running cold water. Sprinkle chicken pieces with salt.
All-purpose flour Vegetable shortening	1¾ quarts As necessary		2. Dredge chicken pieces in flour. Shake off excess flour. 3. Melt shortening in frying pan. Use enough shortening so it is about ⅔ inch deep in pan. Heat shortening so it is hot enough to sizzle but not hot enough to pop or splatter. 4. Place chicken pieces skin-side down in the hot fat. Do not crowd them. Cover pan tightly. Reduce heat to moderate and fry about 15 minutes, checking once or twice to be sure chicken is cooking evenly. 5. Remove frying pan from heat for a moment. Turn chicken over carefully. Return to heat. Cover tightly and fry over moderate heat about 10 minutes or until chicken is well browned. 6. Remove chicken carefully to a steam table pan lined with paper towels. Keep warm until served.
All-purpose flour Milk Salt Pepper	2 cups 1½ gallons As necessary As necessary		7. Pour off all but about 1 cup fat in frying pan. Add flour and cook and stir over moderate heat until flour is lightly browned. Add milk and cook and stir until smooth and thickened. Taste for seasoning. Add salt and pepper if necessary. If the frying pan is not large enough for the gravy,

(continued)

INGREDIENTS	WEIGHTS/MEASURES	FOR ___	METHOD
			scrape browned flour and fat into a saucepan; add milk and cook and stir until gravy is thickened. 8. Serve chicken hot with potatoes or rice. Pour the gravy over the potatoes or rice.

DIETARY INFORMATION:

May be used as written for general and mild 2- to 3-gram sodium-restricted diets.
This recipe provides 3 grams protein per portion.

GIBLET JAMBALAYA
(Acadiana–Cajun)

YIELD: 50 portions (about 2½ gallons)
PAN SIZE: Heavy 3-gallon stockpot
PORTION SIZE: ¾ cup (6 ounces)
TEMPERATURE:

INGREDIENTS	WEIGHTS/MEASURES	FOR ____	METHOD
Shortening Chopped chicken gizzards Chopped onions Chopped fresh green peppers Chopped celery	1 cup 5 pounds 2 cups 1 cup 1 cup		1. Melt shortening over moderate heat in heavy frying pan. Add gizzards, onions, green peppers, and celery. Cook, stirring occasionally, over moderate heat for about 20 minutes or until gizzards are tender.
Chopped chicken livers	5 pounds		2. Add chicken livers to gizzard mixture. Continue to cook, stirring occasionally, over moderate heat for another 10 minutes. Scrape into stockpot.
Canned condensed cream of mushroom soup Uncooked rice Water Salt Black pepper	2½ cups 1¾ quarts (3 pounds) 2¼ quarts ¼ cup 2 tablespoons		3. Add soup, rice, water, salt, and pepper to meat mixture. Cover tightly and simmer 40 minutes, stirring occasionally to keep from sticking.
Chopped parsley	1 cup		4. Stir parsley into jambalaya just before serving. Serve hot.

DIETARY INFORMATION:

May be used as written for general diets.
Diabetic: This recipe provides 3 meat, 1½ bread, and 1 fat exchanges per portion.
This recipe provides 3 ounces protein per portion.

NOTES:

1. This recipe was furnished by Pauline Lalande, R.D., of Lafayette, Louisiana. It was tested and standardized at The Guest Home in Opelousa, Louisiana.
2. Cubed beef, pork, or veal may be used in place of the gizzards and livers but will require more time for cooking in step 1.

Fish

Salmon Pâté 88
Creole Shrimp (Louisiana) 89
   Creole Sauce 90
Shrimp Etouffée (Acadiana–Cajun) 91
Golden Tuna and Noodles 93

SALMON PÂTÉ

YIELD: 2½ quarts   **PORTION SIZE:**
PAN SIZE: **TEMPERATURE:**

INGREDIENTS	WEIGHTS/MEASURES	FOR____	METHOD
Red salmon	1 4-pound can		1. Drain salmon. Remove bones and fat.
Butter or margarine	3 cups (1 pound 8 ounces)		2. Cream butter or margarine about 4 minutes at medium speed. Add lemon pepper or lemon juice and pepper, paprika, monosodium glutamate, and onion powder. Beat at low speed for 1 minute.
Lemon pepper OR	4 teaspoons		
Lemon juice	½ cup		3. Add salmon to creamed mixture. Beat at medium speed for 2 minutes.
Fresh ground black pepper	1 teaspoon		
Paprika	1 tablespoon		
Monosodium glutamate	1 teaspoon		
Onion powder	1 tablespoon		
Finely chopped fresh parsley	¼ cup		4. Line well-buttered mold with parsley. Press pâté into mold and refrigerate until served.
			5. Unmold and garnish as desired. Serve with crackers, toast squares, or Rye Krisp.

DIETARY INFORMATION:

May be used as written for general diets.

CREOLE SHRIMP
(Louisiana)

YIELD: 50 portions (about 2¼ gallons)
PAN SIZE: Heavy 3-gallon stockpot
PORTION SIZE: About ¾ cup over rice
TEMPERATURE:

INGREDIENTS	WEIGHTS/MEASURES	FOR _____	METHOD
Sliced canned mushrooms	1 1-pound can		1. Drain mushrooms. Keep juice for use in step 3.
Chopped onions	2 cups		2. Fry mushrooms, onions, green peppers, and celery in oil in pot over medium heat, stirring occasionally, until onions are limp.
Chopped fresh green peppers	1 cup		
Chopped celery	2 cups		
Vegetable oil	½ cup		
Crushed canned tomatoes and juice	1½ gallons (2 No. 10 cans)		3. Add mushroom juice, tomatoes, salt, pepper, garlic, parsley, and catsup to vegetables. Simmer, uncovered, for one-half hour.
Salt	1½ tablespoons		
Pepper	1 teaspoon		
Minced garlic cloves	8		
Chopped parsley	¼ cup		
Catsup	1 cup		
Melted margarine	¾ cup (1½ sticks)		4. Cook and stir margarine and flour over medium heat until smooth and well browned. Add beef stock and cook and stir until smooth. Add to sauce. Mix lightly and continue to simmer for another 5 minutes.
All-purpose flour	¾ cup		
Beef stock	2 quarts		
Frozen peeled deveined whole raw shrimp or pieces	6 pounds 4 ounces		5. Add thawed shrimp to sauce. Reheat to boiling. Simmer 5 minutes or until shrimp is pink and done. Serve hot over one-half cup rice.
Long-grain rice	1½ quarts (2 pounds 12 ounces)		6. Combine rice, water, salt, and oil in heavy pot. Bring to a boil, stirring occasionally. Cover tightly and simmer 16 minutes. Do not stir. If
Cold water	3 quarts		

(continued)

INGREDIENTS	WEIGHTS/MEASURES	FOR ___	METHOD
Salt Vegetable oil	2 tablespoons 2 tablespoons		rice is not tender, cover and simmer 2 to 3 minutes longer. 7. Uncover rice and allow it to dry and fluff for 3 to 5 minutes.

DIETARY INFORMATION:

May be used as written for general, low-cholesterol and high-fiber diets.
Each portion provides 2 ounces protein.

NOTES:

Variation:
CREOLE SAUCE: Prepare sauce in steps 1 through 4. Use as directed in recipes with chicken, fish, etcetera.

SHRIMP ETOUFFÉE
(Acadiana–Cajun)

YIELD: 50 portions (about 1½ gallons)
PAN SIZE: Heavy 8-quart saucepan
Heavy 3-gallon stockpot

PORTION SIZE: ½ cup (4 ounces) plus ½ cup rice
TEMPERATURE:

INGREDIENTS	WEIGHTS/MEASURES	FOR_____	METHOD
Butter or margarine Chopped onions Finely chopped celery Chopped fresh green peppers	2 cups (1 pound) 2 quarts 1⅓ quarts 2 quarts		1. Melt butter or margarine in saucepan. Add onions, celery and green peppers. Cook over low heat, stirring occasionally, until vegetables are limp.
Tomato paste	1 cup		2. Add tomato paste to vegetables. Mix lightly.
Cornstarch Water	3 tablespoons plus 1 teaspoon 1⅓ quarts		3. Make a smooth paste with a small amount of water and cornstarch. Add with remainder of water to vegetables in saucepan. Mix lightly.
Cleaned raw shrimp	10 pounds		4. Stir shrimp into sauce. Cover and simmer, stirring occasionally, for 5 to 10 minutes or until shrimp are pink and done.
Red pepper Salt Chopped green onion tops	1 tablespoon 1 tablespoon 2 cups		5. Add pepper, salt, and onion tops to etouffée. Serve hot over ½ cup hot rice.
Long-grain rice Cold water Salt Vegetable oil	1½ quarts (2 pounds 12 ounces) 3 quarts 3 tablespoons 2 tablespoons		6. Combine rice, water, salt, and oil in a heavy 3-gallon stockpot. Bring to a boil, stirring occasionally. Cover tightly and simmer 15 minutes without stirring. If rice is not tender, cover and simmer another 2 to 3 minutes. 7. Uncover rice and allow it to dry and fluff for 3 to 5 minutes. Serve hot with etouffée.

(continued)

DIETARY INFORMATION:

May be used as written for general diets for patients accustomed to spicy foods.

Diabetic: This recipe provides 1½ bread, 1½ fat, and 3 meat exchanges per portion.

This recipe provides 3 ounces protein per portion.

NOTES: This recipe was furnished by Della Andreassen, R.D., of Lafayette, Louisiana. It was tested and standardized by Joe Vincent of Heritage Manor, Kaplan, Louisiana.

GOLDEN TUNA AND NOODLES

YIELD: 50 portions (2 pans)
PAN SIZE: 3-gallon stockpot
12 × 20 × 2-inch steam table pans

PORTION SIZE: 3/4 cup (6 ounces)
TEMPERATURE: 375°F Oven

INGREDIENTS	WEIGHTS/MEASURES	FOR _____	METHOD
Homemade noodles	4 pounds		1. Prepare and cook noodles according to recipe on page 118. Drain noodles but do not rinse them. Try to have noodles cooked and hot when sauce is prepared.
Canned tunafish	1 4-pound can		2. Drain tunafish well. Discard oil or water. Put tunafish in mixer bowl. Mix at low speed only until tunafish is broken into small pieces. Keep tunafish for use in step 5.
Chopped celery Chopped onions Margarine or chicken fat All-purpose flour	1 quart 2 cups 1 cup 1 cup		3. Fry celery and onions in margarine or chicken fat over moderate heat, stirring occasionally, until onions are golden in stockpot. Sprinkle flour over vegetables and cook and stir until flour is absorbed.
Lukewarm fat-free chicken broth Salt Pepper	1 gallon As necessary 1/2 teaspoon		4. Add chicken broth to flour mixture. Cook and stir over moderate heat to form a sauce. Add as much salt as necessary and pepper to sauce. 5. Stir tunafish into sauce. 6. Put one-half of the noodles into each of 2 buttered steam table pans. Add one-half of the sauce to each pan. Stir lightly to mix. 7. Bake 30 to 40 minutes or until hot and bubbly. Serve hot.

(continued)

DIETARY INFORMATION:

May be used as written for general diets.
Diabetic: This recipe provides 2 meat, 1 fat, and 1½ bread exchanges per portion, using tuna packed in water.
Low-cholesterol: Use commercial egg noodles in step 1 and margarine instead of chicken fat in step 3.
This recipe provides 2 ounces protein per portion.

NOTES:

1. This recipe was furnished by Hazel Sorensen of Kennedy's Super-Valu Restaurant in Oelwein, Iowa.
2. Homemade style noodles may be purchased commercially in most parts of the country, if desired, or 4 pounds Kluski or egg noodles may be used.

Breads

Baked Brown Bread	97
Baking Powder Biscuits	98
Biscuit Rolls	99
Bran Nut Coffee Cake	100
Light Bran Muffins	101
Date Bran Muffins	101
Raisin Bran Muffins	101
Nut Bran Muffins	101
Dark Raisin Bran Muffins	102
Dark Raisin Bran Loaves	102
Bran Rolls	103
Cinnamon Rolls	105
Cinnamon Raisin Rolls	106
Pecan Rolls	106
Corn Bread (Southern)	107
Cracklin' Bread (Southern)	107
Corn Bread (Yankee)	108
Corn Muffins (Yankee)	108
Corn Bread (Arkansas)	108
Corn Fritters	109
Hush Puppies (Southern)	110
Onion Rolls	111
Snickerdoodle Coffee Cake (Pennsylvania Dutch)	113
Spoonbread (Southern)	114

Information

A bread basket lined with a napkin and filled with an assortment of warm breads indicates immediately to the patron or resident that the management cares about serving quality food. Many good mixes are available as well as excellent brown-and-serve products, but there remains a place in food service for hot breads made on the premises. Preparing yeast or hot breads is not difficult but it does require quality ingredients, attention to recipes, and a thorough understanding of techniques and ingredients.

Flour

Most yeast breads are made from bread flour or all-purpose flour because of their higher gluten content. When whole-wheat, graham, corn, or rye flours are used in yeast breads, they are generally added after the gluten has been developed in the white flour because of their low gluten content. However, flours are combined and added all at once in hot breads because their leavening is provided by baking soda or baking powder and it is not necessary to develop the gluten.

White flour may be stored in a cool dry place but it is important to refrigerate whole-grain flours if not used within a few days to prevent rancidity.

Yeast

Yeast is a living organism which must be kept healthy and alive to rise successfully. Yeast grows best at a temperature of 78°F to 98°F but will die at any temperature over 140°F. Active dry yeast may be stored at room temperature for several months but compressed yeast must be refrigerated until it is used and should not be kept over two to three weeks. Compressed yeast should be dissolved in liquid about 85°F to 87°F, but active dry yeast should be dissolved in liquid about

110°F to 115°F. Some recipes have been developed in which yeast is not dissolved in water but is added to the flour, and the temperature is controlled by adding hot liquid to the flour.

Liquid

It is important to use the right proportion of liquid in relation to the other ingredients in yeast breads. If too little liquid is used, the dough will be heavy and the yeast won't grow as well. If too much liquid is added, the dough will be sticky, hard to handle, and will probably fall when baked. It is difficult to specify the exact amount of liquid which is perfect for a certain amount of flour because some flour absorbs more liquid than others. Therefore, most recipes state a standard amount of liquid and allow a little leeway in the amount of flour used in yeast breads.

Instant Dry Milk

Instant dry milk is used in these recipes because it is convenient and economical. It may be dissolved in water before it is added or it may be combined with dry ingredients. Milk helps soften the texture of yeast breads, gives a browner crust, and helps retain freshness.

Sugar

Sugar provides food for yeast and adds flavor and tenderness to bread. However, a large amount of sugar added to yeast breads will retard the development of the yeast and therefore additional yeast may be necessary in some sweet breads.

Salt

Salt improves the flavor of breads and helps strengthen gluten in yeast breads, but it slows down the action of yeast so it should be added after the yeast has had a chance to develop. Breads made from rye or whole-wheat flour or breads high in milk or shortening need more salt. If salt-free bread is prepared, a salt substitute should be used instead of eliminating salt because the lack of any salt will adversely affect the texture of the bread.

Vegetable Oil

Vegetable oil is used in recipes in this book because it is convenient. easy to measure, doesn't need to be melted, and yields a good product.

Baking Soda

Baking soda is a leavening agent which reacts with acids such as lemon juice, vinegar, molasses, sour milk, buttermilk, or sour cream. Many older recipes include directions for dissolving soda in liquid because it was often caked and hard to use, but this is not necessary now because soda is no longer caked and may be added with other dry ingredients.

Baking Powder

Baking powder is a dry leavening agent which is activated by liquid. Therefore, doughs or batters including baking powder should be baked as soon as possible after liquid and dry ingredients are combined unless the recipe states otherwise. Double-action baking powder was used to test recipes in this book.

BAKED BROWN BREAD

YIELD: 48 portions (4 loaves)
PAN SIZE: 9 × 5 × 3-inch loaf pans
PORTION SIZE: 1 slice
TEMPERATURE: 350°F Oven

INGREDIENTS	WEIGHTS/MEASURES	FOR ___	METHOD
Evaporated milk Water Vinegar	2 cups 2 cups ¼ cup		1. Mix milk, water, and vinegar together. Set aside for use in step 3.
All-purpose flour Whole-wheat flour Sugar Salt Baking soda	1½ quarts 1 quart 2 cups 2 teaspoons 2 tablespoons		2. Place flours, sugar, salt, and baking soda in mixer. Mix at low speed for one-half minute to blend.
Molasses Dark corn syrup Eggs	2 cups 2 cups 1 cup (5 medium)		3. Blend molasses, syrup, and eggs together with milk until smooth. Add all at once to flour mixture. Mix at low speed for one-half minute or only until flour is moistened. 4. Pour one-quarter of the mixture into each of 4 well greased loaf pans. 5. Bake 1 hour or until a cake tester comes out clean. Cool 20 minutes in the pan and then turn out onto a wire rack to cool. 6. Cut each cooled loaf into 12 slices.

DIETARY INFORMATION:

May be used as written for general, soft, bland, and high-fiber diets.

NOTES:

1. One quart molasses may be used instead of the 2 cups each molasses and dark syrup in step 3 if a more pronounced molasses flavor is desired.
2. This bread has a different shape but the same flavor as the traditional round loaves of brown bread.

BAKING POWDER BISCUITS

YIELD: 6 dozen biscuits
PAN SIZE: 18 × 26-inch sheet pans
PORTION SIZE: 1 biscuit
TEMPERATURE: 425°F Oven

INGREDIENTS	WEIGHTS/MEASURES	FOR _____	METHOD
All-purpose flour Instant dry milk Baking powder Salt Shortening	3½ quarts 1⅓ cups ½ cup 1½ tablespoons 3 cups		1. Place flour, dry milk, baking powder, and salt in mixer bowl. Mix 1 minute at low speed to blend. Add shortening and mix at low speed to form a coarse crumb.
Water	About 1½ quarts		2. Add as much of the water as necessary to flour mixture to form a soft dough while beating at low speed. Do not mix any more than absolutely necessary. 3. Turn dough out onto lightly floured working surface. Divide into two equal portions. Knead each portion lightly about 1 minute. 4. Roll dough out to about one-half-inch thickness. Cut with a floured 2½-inch cutter and place on greased sheet pans. Separate biscuits for crusty biscuits and place them close together for soft biscuits. 5. Bake about 15 minutes or until browned.

DIETARY INFORMATION:

May be used as written for general, bland, soft, and mild 2- to 3-gram sodium-restricted diets.

BISCUIT ROLLS

YIELD: 4 dozen rolls
PAN SIZE: 18 × 26-inch sheet pan

PORTION SIZE: 1 roll
TEMPERATURE: 450°F Oven

INGREDIENTS	WEIGHTS/MEASURES	FOR _____	METHOD
Warm water (110-115°F) Active dry yeast Sugar	3¼ cups 1 ounce (3 tablespoons) ¾ cup		1. Combine water, yeast, and sugar; mix lightly. Let stand at room temperature for 10 minutes.
All-purpose flour Nonfat dry milk Baking powder Salt	8½ cups ⅔ cup 2 tablespoons 2 teaspoons		2. Place flour, dry milk, baking powder, and salt in mixer bowl. Mix at low speed for one-half minute to blend.
Shortening	1½ cups		3. Add shortening to flour mixture. Mix at low speed only until mixture resembles coarse crumbs. 4. Using a dough hook, gradually add yeast mixture to flour mixture. Mix at low speed about 1 to 1½ minutes to form a soft dough. 5. Turn dough out onto lightly floured surface. Knead lightly 8 to 10 times. 6. Roll dough out to about one-half-inch thickness. Cut with a 2½-inch cutter. Place biscuits on lightly greased pan. Cover with a cloth and let set 1 hour to 1 hour and 10 minutes at room temperature. 7. Bake 15 minutes or until browned. Serve warm.

DIETARY INFORMATION:

May be used as written for general, bland, soft, and mild 2- to 3-gram sodium-restricted diets.
Diabetic: One-half large or one small biscuit provides 1 bread exchange.

BRAN NUT COFFEE CAKE

YIELD: 54 portions (1 pan)
PAN SIZE: 18 × 26-inch sheet pan

PORTION SIZE: 1 piece
TEMPERATURE: 350°F Oven

INGREDIENTS	WEIGHTS/MEASURES	FOR ___	METHOD
Sugar Brown sugar All-purpose flour Ground cinnamon Softened margarine Chopped nuts	2/3 cup 2 cups 1/4 cup 2 tablespoons 3/4 cup (1 1/2 sticks) 1 1/4 cups		1. Mix sugars, flour, cinnamon, margarine, and nuts together to form a coarse crumb. Set aside for use in step 6.
Shortening Sugar Vanilla	3 cups 3 cups 1 tablespoon		2. Cream shortening, sugar, and vanilla together until light and fluffy.
Eggs	2/3 cup (about 4 medium)		3. Add eggs to creamed mixture. Beat at low speed for 1 minute or until well-blended.
All-purpose flour Baking powder Salt	1 1/2 quarts 3 tablespoons 1 1/2 teaspoons		4. Stir flour, baking powder, and salt together to blend.
All Bran or Bran Buds Milk	3 cups 3 cups		5. Combine bran and milk. Mix well. Add with flour to creamed mixture. Mix at low speed only until flour is moistened. 6. Spread batter in greased sheet pan. Sprinkle topping over batter. Press topping lightly into batter. 7. Bake 30 to 35 minutes or until cake springs back when touched in the center. 8. Cut 6 × 9 and serve warm if possible.

DIETARY INFORMATION:

May be used as written for general and high-fiber diets.

LIGHT BRAN MUFFINS

YIELD: 4 dozen medium size muffins
PAN SIZE: 12-cup muffin tins
PORTION SIZE: 1 muffin
TEMPERATURE: 400°F Oven

INGREDIENTS	WEIGHTS/MEASURES	FOR ___	METHOD
Water Sugar Vegetable oil Nonfat dry milk Eggs Salt	1 quart 1 cup 1 cup 1 cup ¾ cup (3 to 4 medium) 1 teaspoon		1. Place water, sugar, oil, dry milk, eggs, and salt in mixer bowl; beat at medium speed for one-half minute or until well blended.
All-purpose flour Baking powder All Bran or Bran Buds	4½ cups 3 tablespoons 1½ quarts		2. Stir flour and baking powder together until well blended; add bran and mix lightly; add to liquid in mixer bowl and mix at low speed only until flour is moistened. 3. Put a level No. 20 dipper of batter in each greased or paper-lined muffin cup. (You should work as quickly as possible to avoid having the bran blend into the batter.) 4. Bake 25 to 30 minutes. Serve warm if possible.

DIETARY INFORMATION:

May be used as written for general, high-fiber, and mild 2- to 3-gram sodium-restricted diets.

NOTES: Silicone-treated paper liners for muffin cups make it easier to remove the muffins from the tins and the paper from the muffins.

Variations:
1. *DATE BRAN MUFFINS:* Add 3 cups chopped dates with the dry ingredients in step 2.
2. *RAISIN BRAN MUFFINS:* Add 3 cups washed and drained raisins with the dry ingredients in step 2.
3. *NUT BRAN MUFFINS:* Add 3 cups chopped nuts with the dry ingredients in step 2.

DARK RAISIN BRAN MUFFINS

YIELD: 6 dozen muffins
PAN SIZE: 12-cup muffin tins
PORTION SIZE: 1 muffin
TEMPERATURE: 400°F Oven

INGREDIENTS	WEIGHTS/MEASURES	FOR ___	METHOD
All-purpose flour Salt Baking soda	1½ quarts 1 tablespoon 2 tablespoons		1. Place flour, salt, and baking soda in mixer bowl. Mix one-half minute at low speed to blend.
All Bran or Bran Buds Raisins	2¼ quarts 3 cups		2. Add bran and raisins to flour mixture. Mix one-half minute at low speed to blend.
Eggs Sugar Molasses Sour milk or buttermilk Vegetable oil	1 cup (about 5 medium) 2 cups 1 cup 1½ quarts ¾ cup		3. Beat eggs, sugar, molasses, milk, and oil together to blend. Add to flour mixture. Mix 1 minute at low speed. 4. Use a No. 20 dipper to fill muffin cups two-thirds full. 5. Bake 20 to 25 minutes or until muffins spring back when touched in the center. Serve warm if possible.

DIETARY INFORMATION:

May be used as written for general and high-fiber diets.

NOTES: Silicone-treated paper liners for muffin cups make it easier to remove the muffins from the tins and the paper from the muffins.

Variation:

DARK RAISIN BRAN LOAVES: Put one-quarter of the batter into each of 4 well-buttered 9 × 5 × 3-inch loaf pans. Bake 40 to 50 minutes or until loaf springs back when touched in the center. Cool 10 minutes in the pan. Remove and cool to room temperature before slicing.

BRAN ROLLS

YIELD: 5 dozen rolls
PAN SIZE: 18 × 26-inch sheet pans
PORTION SIZE: 1 roll
TEMPERATURE: 375°F Oven

INGREDIENTS	WEIGHTS/MEASURES	FOR_____	METHOD
Hot water Nonfat dry milk Brown sugar Bran Buds or All Bran	1 quart 1 1/3 cups 2/3 cup 2 cups		1. Place water, dry milk, sugar, and bran in mixer bowl. Mix at low speed for one-half minute. Cool to lukewarm, about 85° to 87°F.
Compressed yeast	3 ounces		2. Crumble yeast and add to liquid. Let stand 5 to 10 minutes.
All-purpose flour	1 quart		3. Add flour to liquid. Beat at low speed using dough hook for 6 to 8 minutes.
Vegetable oil Salt	1/2 cup 1 tablespoon		4. Add oil and salt to batter. Beat at low speed for 1 minute.
All-purpose flour Vegetable oil	1 to 1 1/2 quarts 2 tablespoons		5. Add 2 cups of the flour to the dough. Beat 1 minute at low speed. Turn dough out onto a surface covered with the remaining 1 quart of flour. Knead as much of the flour as necessary into the dough to make a smooth elastic dough. Form dough into a round ball and place in a well greased bowl. Spread the top lightly with oil. Cover with a cloth and let stand in a warm place until doubled in volume. 6. Return dough to lightly floured surface and knead lightly for 1 minute. Return to bowl. Spread lightly with oil. Cover and let rise again until doubled in volume. 7. Turn dough out onto lightly floured surface. Knead lightly and then divide dough into 5 equal portions of about 1 pound 8 ounces each. Round

(continued)

INGREDIENTS	WEIGHTS/MEASURES	FOR _____	METHOD
			each portion into a ball. Cover with a cloth and let stand 10 to 15 minutes. 8. Roll each ball into a roll about 16 inches long. Cut each roll into 12 equal portions. Shape as desired and place on lightly greased sheet pans. Cover and let rise again until doubled in volume. 9. Bake 30 to 40 minutes or until well browned. Serve warm, if possible.

DIETARY INFORMATION:

May be used as written for general, high-fiber, bland, low-cholesterol, low-fat, and mild 2- to 3-gram sodium-restricted diets.

CINNAMON ROLLS

YIELD: 4 dozen rolls
PAN SIZE: 18 × 26-inch sheet pan
PORTION SIZE: 1 roll
TEMPERATURE: 375°F Oven

INGREDIENTS	WEIGHTS/MEASURES	FOR ___	METHOD
Very hot water Sugar Nonfat dry milk	2½ cups 2 cups ¾ cup		1. Place water, sugar, and dry milk in mixer bowl. Mix at low speed until sugar is dissolved. Cool to lukewarm, about 85° to 87°F.
Compressed yeast	3 ounces		2. Crumble yeast into milk mixture. Mix briefly at low speed and let stand 5 to 10 minutes.
All-purpose flour	1 quart		3. Add flour to liquid and beat at low speed, using a dough hook, for 5 minutes.
All-purpose flour Softened margarine Eggs Salt	1 quart 1 cup (2 sticks) 1 cup (5 medium) 1 tablespoon		4. Add flour, margarine, eggs, and salt to dough. Beat at low speed for 3 minutes or until well mixed.
All-purpose flour Vegetable oil	2 cups 2 tablespoons		5. Turn dough out onto a working surface covered with the 2 cups of flour. Knead as much of the flour into the dough as necessary to make a smooth elastic dough. Shape dough into a round ball and place in a well greased bowl. Spread the top lightly with oil. Cover with a cloth and let stand in a warm place until doubled in volume. 6. Turn dough out onto lightly floured working surface. Knead 2 minutes and return to bowl. Brush top of dough with oil. Cover with a cloth and let rise until doubled in volume. 7. Turn dough out onto lightly floured working surface. Divide dough into 2 equal portions of about 3 pounds 4 ounces each. Cover with a cloth and let stand 10 minutes.

(continued)

INGREDIENTS	WEIGHTS/MEASURES	FOR ___
Softened margarine	½ cup (1 stick)	
Brown sugar	1½ cups	
Sugar	1½ cups	
Ground cinnamon	2 tablespoons	

METHOD

8. Use about one-half of the margarine to heavily grease a sheet pan. Mix sugars and cinnamon and sprinkle one-half of the sugar mixture over the margarine in the sheet pan.
9. Roll each ball of dough into a 9 × 16-inch rectangle. Spread one-half of the remaining margarine evenly on each piece of dough.
10. Sprinkle one-half of the remaining sugar mixture evenly over the margarine on each rectangle. Roll into long rolls and cut each roll like a jelly roll into 24 equal slices.
11. Put sliced rolls 6 × 8 on top of sugar mixture in sheet pan. Cover with a cloth and let rise until doubled in volume.
12. Bake 30 to 35 minutes or until golden brown.
13. Turn rolls out and upside down immediately. Serve warm if possible.

DIETARY INFORMATION:

May be used as written for general, bland, soft, and mild 2- to 3-gram sodium-restricted diets.

NOTES:

Variations:
1. *CINNAMON RAISIN ROLLS:* Sprinkle 1½ cups washed and drained raisins over sugar mixture on rectangles before rolling and cutting.
2. *PECAN ROLLS:* Sprinkle 3 cups coarsely chopped pecans over sugar in sheet pan before putting sliced rolls on the sugar mixture.

CORN BREAD
(Southern)

YIELD: 54 portions (1 pan)
PAN SIZE: 18 × 26-inch sheet pan
PORTION SIZE: 1 slice
TEMPERATURE: 425°F Oven

INGREDIENTS	WEIGHTS/MEASURES	FOR ___	METHOD
Yellow or white cornmeal All-purpose flour Sugar Baking powder Baking soda Salt	3 quarts 3 cups ¼ cup ¼ cup 1 tablespoon 1 tablespoon		1. Place cornmeal, flour, sugar, baking powder, soda, and salt in mixer bowl. Mix at low speed for 1 minute to blend.
Buttermilk or sour milk Eggs Melted bacon fat or vegetable oil	2 quarts 2 cups (10 medium) 1¼ cups		2. Beat milk, eggs, and fat together until smooth. Add all at once to cornmeal mixture. Mix at low speed only until cornmeal is moistened. 3. Spread batter in sheet pan which has been heavily greased with bacon fat or shortening. Bake 30 to 35 minutes or until firm. 4. Cut 6 × 9 and serve warm.

DIETARY INFORMATION:

May be used as written for general, high-fiber, bland, and soft diets.

Diabetic: 1 ounce serving provides 1 bread exchange.

NOTES:

Variation:
CRACKLIN' BREAD (Southern): Fry 1 pound chopped bacon until crisp. Drain well. Add cooked bacon to the batter in step 2.

CORN BREAD
(Yankee)

YIELD: 54 portions (1 pan)
PAN SIZE: 18 × 26-inch sheet pan
PORTION SIZE: 1 slice
TEMPERATURE: 400°F Oven

INGREDIENTS	WEIGHTS/MEASURES	FOR ___	METHOD
All-purpose flour Yellow cornmeal Nonfat dry milk Sugar Baking powder Salt	2 quarts 2 quarts 2 cups 2 cups 6 tablespoons 1½ tablespoons		1. Place flour, cornmeal, dry milk, sugar, baking powder, and salt in mixer bowl. Mix one-half minute at low speed to blend.
Eggs Water Vegetable oil	1½ cups (7 to 8 medium) 2 quarts 2 cups		2. Mix eggs, water, and oil together to blend. Add all at once to flour mixture. Mix at low speed only until flour is moistened. 3. Spread batter evenly in well greased pan. Bake 30 to 35 minutes or until lightly browned and firm. 4. Cut 6 × 9 and serve hot, if possible.

DIETARY INFORMATION:

May be used as written for general, high-fiber, bland, and soft diets.

Diabetic: 1 ounce serving provides 1 bread exchange.

NOTES:

Variations:
1. *CORN MUFFINS (Yankee):* Fill each muffin tin two-thirds full using a No. 20 dipper. Bake about 25 minutes or until lightly browned. Basic recipe yields 8 dozen muffins. Silicone-treated paper liners for muffin cups makes it easier to remove the muffins from the tins and the paper from the muffins.
2. *CORN BREAD (Arkansas):* Use ¼ cup sugar instead of 2 cups in step 1. Delete vegetable oil and substitute 2 cups melted bacon fat in step 2. This corn bread will not be as brown as the basic corn bread.

CORN FRITTERS

YIELD: 50 portions (about 100 fritters)
PAN SIZE:

PORTION SIZE: 2 fritters
TEMPERATURE: 350°F Hot fat, 275°F Oven

INGREDIENTS	WEIGHTS/MEASURES	FOR ____	METHOD
All-purpose flour Salt Baking powder Sugar Nonfat dry milk	2¼ quarts 1 tablespoon 6 tablespoons ¼ cup ½ cup		1. Place flour, salt, baking powder, sugar, and dry milk in mixer bowl. Mix at low speed for one-half minute to blend.
Warm water Eggs Vegetable oil	1½ cups 1½ cups (7 to 8 medium) ½ cup		2. Beat water, eggs, and oil together until smooth.
Cream-style corn Drained whole-kernel corn	4½ cups 1 quart		3. Stir corns into egg mixture. Add all at once to flour mixture. Mix at low speed only until flour is moistened. 4. Drop by heaping tablespoon (rounded No. 40 dipper) into hot fat. Fry about 5 minutes or until browned. Drain on brown paper or paper towels. 5. Serve hot with syrup immediately or keep warm in a paper-towel-lined steam table pan in the oven.

DIETARY INFORMATION:

May be used as written for general, bland, and mild 2- to 3-gram sodium-restricted diets.

HUSH PUPPIES
(Southern)

YIELD: 50 portions (100 hush puppies)
PAN SIZE:

PORTION SIZE: 2 hush puppies
TEMPERATURE: 375°F Hot fat, 275°F Oven

INGREDIENTS	WEIGHTS/MEASURES	FOR ___	METHOD
All-purpose flour Cornmeal Nonfat dry milk Baking powder Salt Pepper	4½ cups 1¼ quarts 1 cup 3 tablespoons 2 teaspoons ½ teaspoon		1. Place flour, cornmeal, dry milk, baking powder, salt, and pepper in mixer bowl. Mix at low speed for one-half minute to blend.
Eggs Water Melted bacon fat or shortening Finely chopped onions	1½ cups (7 to 8 medium) 1 quart 1 cup 3 cups		2. Mix eggs, water, and fat together until smooth. Add along with onions to flour mixture. Mix at low speed only until flour is moistened. 3. Drop by level No. 30 (2 tablespoons) dipper into hot fat. Fry for 4 to 5 minutes or until well browned. 4. Serve hot with fish or seafood immediately or keep warm in a paper-towel-lined steam table pan in the oven.

DIETARY INFORMATION:

May be used as written for general and high-fiber diets.

ONION ROLLS

YIELD: 6 dozen rolls
PAN SIZE: 18 × 26-inch sheet pans

PORTION SIZE: 1 roll
TEMPERATURE: 425°F Oven

INGREDIENTS	WEIGHTS/MEASURES	FOR _____	METHOD
Very hot water Sugar Nonfat dry milk	1½ quarts ½ cup ⅔ cup		1. Place water, sugar, and dry milk in mixer bowl. Mix at low speed until sugar is dissolved. Cool to 105° to 110°F.
Active dry yeast	¼ cup (1⅓ ounces)		2. Stir yeast into liquid. Mix a few seconds at low speed. Let stand 5 to 10 minutes.
All-purpose flour	2 quarts		3. Add flour to liquid and beat at low speed using a dough hook for about 5 minutes.
Salt Vegetable oil	3 tablespoons ½ cup		4. Add salt and oil to batter. Mix at low speed for 1 minute.
Finely chopped onions	1 quart		5. Remove any excess moisture from onions by draining them well and then pressing out any remaining juice by pushing them against the side of a strainer with the back of a large spoon. 6. Add onions to batter. Mix 1 minute at low speed.
All-purpose flour Vegetable oil	2 quarts 2 tablespoons		7. Add 1 quart of flour to the batter. Beat 1 minute at low speed. Turn dough out onto a working surface covered with the remaining 1 quart flour. Knead as much of the flour as necessary into the dough to make a smooth elastic dough. 8. Form dough into a round ball and place in a well greased bowl. Spread the top lightly with oil. Cover with a cloth and let stand in a warm place until doubled in volume. 9. Return dough to lightly floured surface and knead lightly for 1 minute. Return to bowl. Spread

(continued)

INGREDIENTS	WEIGHTS/MEASURES	FOR_____	METHOD
			lightly with oil. Cover and let rise again until doubled in volume. 10. Turn dough out onto lightly floured working surface. Knead lightly and then divide dough into 6 equal portions of about 1 pound 11 ounces each. Round each portion into a ball. Cover with a cloth and let stand 10 to 15 minutes. 11. Roll each ball into a roll about 16 inches long. Cut each roll into 12 equal portions. Round each roll and place 9 × 4 on lightly greased sheet pans. Cover and let rise again until doubled in volume. 12. Bake about 15 minutes or until browned. Serve warm if possible

DIETARY INFORMATION:

May be used as written for general, bland, low-cholesterol, and mild 2- to 3-gram sodium-restricted diets.

Diabetic: Each roll provides 2 bread exchanges.

SNICKERDOODLE COFFEE CAKE
(Pennsylvania Dutch)

YIELD: 54 portions (1 pan)
PAN SIZE: 18 × 26-inch sheet pan
PORTION SIZE: 1 piece
TEMPERATURE: 375°F Oven

INGREDIENTS	WEIGHTS/MEASURES	FOR _____	METHOD
Brown sugar Margarine All-purpose flour Ground cinnamon	2 cups ¾ cup (1½ sticks) ½ cup 2 tablespoons		1. Mix sugar, margarine, flour, and cinnamon together to form a coarse crumb. Set aside for use in step 6.
Cake flour Baking powder Nonfat dry milk Ground nutmeg Salt	2¼ quarts 3 tablespoons ½ cup 1½ teaspoons 1½ teaspoons		2. Place flour, baking powder, dry milk, nutmeg, and salt in mixer bowl. Mix at low speed for one-half minute to blend.
Washed and drained raisins Chopped nuts	2½ cups 2 cups		3. Add raisins and nuts to flour mixture. Mix at low speed about one-half minute to coat raisins and nuts with flour mixture.
Shortening Sugar Eggs Vanilla	1¼ cups 3½ cups 1 cup (about 5 medium) 1 tablespoon		4. Cream shortening and sugar together until fluffy. Add eggs and vanilla. Beat 1 minute at medium speed.
Water	2 cups		5. Add all of the flour mixture and then all of the water to the creamed mixture. Mix at low speed only until flour is moistened. Spread batter in lightly greased pan. 6. Spread crumb topping on batter. Press lightly. 7. Bake 30 to 35 minutes or until lightly browned and the center springs back when touched. 8. Cut 6 × 9 and serve warm if possible.

DIETARY INFORMATION:

May be used as written for general diets.

SPOONBREAD
(Southern)

YIELD: 48 portions (2 pans)
PAN SIZE: 12 × 20 × 2-inch steam table pans
Heavy 3-gallon stockpot
PORTION SIZE: 1 piece
TEMPERATURE: 375°F Oven

INGREDIENTS	WEIGHTS/MEASURES	FOR ___	METHOD
Milk Cornmeal Salt	4½ quarts 1½ quarts (2 pounds) 3 tablespoons		1. Put milk in stockpot. Stir cornmeal and salt into milk. Cook over medium heat, stirring constantly, until thickened to the consistency of cornmeal mush. Remove from heat.
Butter or margarine	¾ cup (1½ sticks)		2. Stir butter or margarine into hot cornmeal mixture. Cool to lukewarm.
Beaten egg yolks	2 cups (about 24 medium)		3. Stir egg yolks into cornmeal mixture. Mix well.
Egg whites	3 cups (about 24 medium)		4. Beat egg whites until stiff but not dry. Fold into cornmeal mixture. 5. Pour one-half of the batter (about 1¼ gallons) into each of two buttered steam table pans. 6. Bake about 45 minutes or until set. Cut each pan 3 × 8 and serve hot. Spoonbread falls after it has set and cooled so it should be prepared as close to serving time as possible.

DIETARY INFORMATION:

May be used as written for general, high-fiber, soft, and bland diets.

Potato Substitutes

Fried Cornmeal Mush (New England) 116
Hominy Grits (Southern) 117
Caraway Noodles (Minnesota) 118
Homemade Noodles 119
Fruit Rice 121
Steamed Rice 122

FRIED CORNMEAL MUSH
(New England)

YIELD: 50 portions (about 2 gallons)
PAN SIZE: Heavy 3-gallon stockpot
9 × 5 × 3-inch bread pans

PORTION SIZE: 3 slices (about $\frac{2}{3}$ cup)
TEMPERATURE: 400°F Grill

INGREDIENTS	WEIGHTS/MEASURES	FOR _____	METHOD
Butter or margarine Salt Water	$\frac{1}{2}$ cup (1 stick) $1\frac{1}{2}$ tablespoons $1\frac{1}{2}$ gallons		1. Combine butter or margarine, salt, and water in stockpot. Cover and bring to a boil.
Cornmeal Cold water	3 pounds ($1\frac{3}{4}$ quarts) 2 quarts		2. Combine cornmeal and water. Stir until smooth. Pour slowly into boiling water, stirring constantly. Cook, stirring constantly, over medium heat until smooth and thickened. Reduce heat to very low and continue to cook, stirring frequently, for another 25 to 30 minutes. 3. Pour about 1 quart of mush into each of 8 bread pans. Press plastic wrap over mush in each loaf pan which has cooled slightly. Refrigerate overnight or until chilled and firm. Turn loaves out onto a slicing board and slice each loaf into eighteen $\frac{1}{2}$-inch slices.
All-purpose flour Warmed syrup	As necessary As necessary		4. Dip each slice lightly in flour and fry about 8 minutes on each side or until browned on well-greased griddle. Serve hot with warmed syrup. (Slices may be kept warm until serving by putting them shingle-style in a steam table pan in a 200°F oven.)

DIETARY INFORMATION:

May be used as written for general diets. For mild 2- to 3-gram sodium-restricted diets fry mush in vegetable oil or salt-free butter or margarine.
Diabetic: This recipe provides $1\frac{1}{2}$ bread exchanges per portion, plus fat used for frying the mush. Serve special syrup made with sugar substitute.
Low-cholesterol: Fry mush in margarine or vegetable oil and use margarine in step 1.

NOTES:
Variation:
CORNMEAL MUSH: Serve about $\frac{2}{3}$ cup hot mush in a bowl with milk and sugar or with butter or margarine and sugar.

HOMINY GRITS
(Southern)

YIELD: 50 portions (about 2¼ gallons)
PAN SIZE: Heavy 5-gallon stockpot
9 × 5 × 3-inch bread pans

PORTION SIZE: ¾ cup (6 ounces)
TEMPERATURE: 400°F Grill

INGREDIENTS	WEIGHTS/MEASURES	FOR_____	METHOD
REGULAR Hominy grits Salt Boiling water	 3 pounds 4 ounces 3 tablespoons 3 gallons		1. Pour grits slowly into boiling salted water, stirring constantly. Cover and simmer 25 to 30 minutes, stirring occasionally. Serve hot.
QUICK Hominy grits Salt Boiling water	 3 pounds 3 tablespoons 2¼ gallons		1. Pour grits into boiling salted water, stirring constantly. Simmer 7 to 10 minutes over low heat, stirring frequently. 2. Remove from heat. Cover and let stand 5 minutes. Serve hot.
FRIED HOMINY GRITS Recipe of hominy grits All-purpose flour	 See above As necessary		1. Pour about 1 quart hot cooked grits into each of eight 9 × 5 × 3-inch bread pans. Cool slightly. Press plastic wrap over grits in each pan. Refrigerate overnight or until chilled and firm. Turn loaves out onto a slicing board and slice each loaf into eighteen ½-inch slices. 2. Dip each slice lightly in flour. Fry about 8 minutes on each side or until lightly browned on well greased griddle. Serve hot, 3 slices per serving.

DIETARY INFORMATION:

May be used as written for general and mild 2- to 3-gram sodium-restricted diets.
Diabetic: This recipe provides 1½ bread exchanges per portion, plus fat used for Fried Hominy Grits.
Low-cholesterol: Fry grits in margarine or vegetable oil.
Regular or Quick Hominy Grits may also be used as written for low-sodium, bland, and low-fat diets.

CARAWAY NOODLES
(Minnesota)

YIELD: 50 portions (about 1½ gallons)
PAN SIZE: Heavy 5-gallon stockpot
PORTION SIZE: ½ cup (4 ounces)
TEMPERATURE:

INGREDIENTS	WEIGHTS/MEASURES	FOR ___	METHOD
Egg noodles Hot water Salt Vegetable oil	3 pounds 3 gallons 3 tablespoons 2 tablespoons		1. Stir noodles into boiling salted water. Add oil and cook 10 to 12 minutes or until noodles are tender, stirring occasionally. 2. Drain well.
Caraway seeds Slivered almonds	⅓ cup 3 cups (12 ounces)		3. While noodles are cooking, place seeds and almonds in a dry frying pan and toast, stirring occasionally, over medium heat until seeds and nuts are golden.
Melted butter or margarine	1½ cups (3 sticks)		4. Toss seeds, almonds, melted butter or margarine, and hot noodles together. Serve hot with roast pork or pork chops.

DIETARY INFORMATION:

May be used as written for general and mild 2- to 3-gram sodium-restricted diets.
Diabetic: This recipe provides 2 fat and ½ bread exchanges per portion.

HOMEMADE NOODLES

YIELD: 50 portions (about 1½ gallons)
PAN SIZE: Heavy 3-gallon stockpot
PORTION SIZE: ½ cup (about 3 ounces)
TEMPERATURE:

INGREDIENTS	WEIGHTS/MEASURES	FOR _____	METHOD
Egg yolks	1½ cups (18 to 21 medium)		1. Combine egg yolks, whole eggs, salt, and water. Beat at low speed until smooth but not foamy.
Whole eggs	1 cup (about 5 medium)		2. Place 10 cups of flour in mixer bowl. Add egg mixture and mix at low speed, using dough hook, about 3 minutes or until dough forms a smooth ball and leaves the sides of the bowl. Beat another 2 minutes at low speed. Add as much of the remaining flour as necessary to form a smooth rather firm dough. The amount of flour needed will depend upon the brand of flour used.
Salt	4 teaspoons		
Water	1½ cups		
All-purpose flour	10½ to 11 cups		

OR

Sift all of the flour into a mound on a working surface. Make a well in the center of the flour and pour the egg mixture into it. Mix the egg mixture into the flour, a little at a time, until the flour is all absorbed and the flour and egg mixture are well blended. Add a little more water, 1 tablespoon at a time, if necessary, to absorb most of the flour. Knead the dough lightly on a floured working surface about 10 minutes or until it is smooth and resilient.

3. Cover dough with a clean cloth and let it stand 30 minutes at room temperature.
4. Divide noodles into 4 equal portions. Roll each portion ⅛- to ¼-inch thick as you would roll out pie crust. Roll each portion into a loose roll like a jelly roll without any filling and slice ⅛- to ¼-inch wide, using a very sharp knife, depending upon how they are to be used. Sprinkle

(continued)

INGREDIENTS	WEIGHTS/MEASURES	FOR _____	METHOD
			dough very lightly with flour as it is rolled to make it easier to separate the noodles after they are cut.
Boiling water or broth Salt Margarine or vegetable oil	2 gallons 1½ tablespoons 1 tablespoon		5. Drop noodles into boiling salted water or broth. Do not add salt if seasoned broth is used. Stir noodles gently until water or broth has started to boil again. Add margarine or oil and continue to cook over moderate heat, stirring occasionally, about 15 to 20 minutes or until tender. Drain well and serve hot as a side dish or combine with other ingredients as directed in a specific recipe.

DIETARY INFORMATION:

May be used as written for general, bland, soft, low-fat, and mild 2- to 3-gram sodium-restricted diets.
Diabetic: This recipe provides ½ meat, ½ fat, and 1½ bread exchanges per portion.

FRUIT RICE

YIELD: 50 portions (about 1½ gallons)
PAN SIZE: Heavy 8-quart pot

PORTION SIZE: ½ cup (No. 8 dipper)
TEMPERATURE:

INGREDIENTS	WEIGHTS/MEASURES	FOR ___	METHOD
Long-grain rice Margarine	1½ quarts (2 pounds 12 ounces) 1 cup (2 sticks)		1. Fry rice in pot in margarine over medium heat, stirring frequently, for 3 to 5 minutes or until grains of rice are glistening and have a milky look.
Hot fat-free chicken broth Pepper Powdered thyme Powdered rosemary Salt	3 quarts ½ teaspoon 1 teaspoon ½ teaspoon As necessary		2. Combine broth, pepper, thyme, and rosemary. Taste for seasoning and add more salt if necessary. Add stock to rice. Stir to mix well. Bring to a boil. Cover, reduce heat, and simmer 16 minutes. Taste rice for tenderness. If rice is not tender, return to heat and cook 2 to 3 minutes longer. 3. Remove from heat. Uncover and fluff with a fork. Let stand 2 to 3 minutes to dry.
Fruit cocktail and juice Raisins	1 quart 1 cup		4. Heat fruit cocktail and raisins together. Drain well and add warm to rice. Toss lightly and serve hot.

DIETARY INFORMATION:

May be used as written for general and low-cholesterol diets.

NOTES: Chopped drained apricots, pineapple, or other fruits may be used in place of fruit cocktail.

STEAMED RICE

YIELD: 50 portions (about 1½ gallons)
PAN SIZE: Heavy 3-gallon stockpot

PORTION SIZE: ½ cup (No. 8 dipper)
TEMPERATURE:

INGREDIENTS	WEIGHTS/MEASURES	FOR _____	METHOD
Long-grain rice	1½ quarts (2 pounds 12 ounces)		1. Combine rice, water, salt, and oil in stockpot. Bring to a boil stirring occasionally. Cover tightly, reduce heat, and simmer 15 minutes. Do not stir. If rice is not tender, return to heat. Cover and simmer 2 to 3 minutes longer.
Cold water	3 quarts		2. Uncover rice. Remove from heat and allow rice to fluff and dry 3 to 5 minutes before it is served.
Salt	2 tablespoons		
Vegetable oil	2 tablespoons		

DIETARY INFORMATION:

May be used for general, soft, low-fat, low-cholesterol, bland, and mild 2- to 3-gram sodium-restricted diets.

Diabetic: This recipe provides 1 bread exchange per portion.

Salads

Avocado Green Salad (California)	125
Guacamole (Southwestern)	126
Celery Slaw (Florida)	127
Cole Slaw	128
Carrot and Cabbage Slaw	128
Molded Cole Slaw	129
Cranberry Relish (New England)	130
Cucumber Lettuce Salad (Midwestern)	131
Frijole Salad (Southwestern)	132
Frijole Lettuce Salad	132
Wilted Lettuce (Midwestern and Pennsylvania Dutch)	133
Lima Bean Salad	134
Macaroni Slaw (Midwestern)	135
Grated Potato Salad (Midwestern)	136
Sauerkraut Salad	137
Molded Strawberries and Cream Cheese (Midwestern)	138
Salad Dressing for Vegetables	139

Information

Salads, which add both texture and nutrition to the meal, are an important part of the American diet. Since they are so important, they should be fresh, crisp, and colorful. They should be served on or in cold dishes and should be garnished attractively when appropriate. Dressings should not be added until the last moment unless they are a part of the salad as in cole slaw or a marinated vegetable salad.

Salad Greens

1. A good tossed salad begins with clean, crisp, cold greens. Greens lose texture and nutrients from day to day even when kept under proper refrigeration. Salad greens are fragile and must be stored carefully. Do not wash or trim greens or remove them from their containers unless they are to be used within 24 hours. Wash and trim greens as soon as possible after they are removed from their shipping container. Do not allow them to stand at room temperature any longer than necessary. They should be refrigerated until cleaned and then returned to the refrigerator as promptly as possible.

2. Cleaning Salad Greens:
   a. Fill a sink full of lukewarm water or cool water. Add some salt to help get rid of insects and, if two sinks are available, fill the second sink with cool water.
   b. Discard any damaged outer leaves but keep as many of them as possible for their color and higher Vitamin A content. Leave lettuce whole except for removing the core. Separate leaves of romaine or escarole, place the leaves in the water, and discard the core.
   c. Soak greens in the first sink for about 15 minutes. Give the leaves plenty of room in the sink. Wash them by lifting them up and down in the sink and then put them in the second sink. Never leave the greens in the sink and run the water out of the sink. The water and any dirt or insects should be left in the sink after you remove the greens.
   d. Soak greens in the second sink for about 15 minutes also and then lift them up and down to wash them. They should be drained in a large colander or rack on the drain board. Greens should be drained well with just a little bit of water clinging to them. Refrigerate greens an hour or so after they are washed before they are used to allow them to crisp. They can be stored in a big plastic bag or in a steam table pan with a damp cloth or plastic over them.

3. Salad greens should be torn instead of cut with a knife unless they are to be shredded, in which case a knife must be used.
4. Salad dressing should not be added to greens until just before they are served. If they are served on a buffet, the dressing should be served separately.

Molded (Gelatin) Salads

1. Molded salads should always be served chilled on chilled plates, and should never be allowed to stand in a warm room.
2. Fruit-flavored gelatin must be thoroughly dissolved in hot liquid, generally water or fruit juice, before cold water or fruit juice is added. The amount of liquid specified in the recipe should always be used, since gelatin with too little liquid will be hard and rubbery and gelatin with too much liquid will be soft and will never set.
3. Fruits will be more evenly distributed throughout the gelatin if they are not added until the gelatin is partially firm.
4. Fresh pineapple should never be added to a gelatin salad, since an enzyme in the pineapple prevents the hardening of the gelatin salad.
5. Diabetic gelatin should be made from diabetic fruit-flavored gelatin and diabetic fruits. Free vegetables such as cabbage and cucumbers or a free fruit such as rhubarb may be used in diabetic gelatin for a free salad, but other ingredients that are counted in a diabetic diet must be counted when added to salads.

Fruit Salads

1. Fruit salads should always be served chilled on chilled plates, and should never be allowed to sit in a warm room.
2. Canned fruits should be well drained before they are combined in a fruit salad. The fruit juice should be saved for use in gelatin, as a beverage, or in a sauce.
3. Fresh fruits will retain their color and not turn brown if they are dropped into fruit juice with acid in it such as pineapple or orange juice or into water with lemon juice in it when they are being prepared. They should be well drained before they are combined with other fruits.
4. Fresh fruits for salads or other uses, except bananas, should be refrigerated until used.
5. Fresh fruits should be thoroughly washed and drained and any bruised spots removed before they are prepared for use in salads.
6. The use of prepared orange and grapefruit segments is generally less expensive than the use of fresh segments prepared in the kitchen.

AVOCADO GREEN SALAD
(California)

YIELD: 50 portions (about 3 gallons)
PAN SIZE:

PORTION SIZE: 1 cup
TEMPERATURE:

INGREDIENTS	WEIGHTS/MEASURES	FOR ____	METHOD
Shredded lettuce	1¾ gallons (about 3 pounds 8 ounces)		1. Put lettuce in large mixing bowl.
Avocados Salt Lemon juice	3 pounds 1½ teaspoons ¼ cup		2. Peel avocados. Remove seeds and slice into ¼-inch slices. Sprinkle with salt and lemon juice and place on top of lettuce.
Fresh tomatoes Chopped fresh green peppers Chopped celery Choice of salad dressings	2 pounds 3 cups 3 cups As necessary		3. Wash and core tomatoes. Remove cores and cut into about 8 wedges each. Place on top of avocado slices. 4. Add peppers and celery to salad. Toss lightly and serve with a choice of salad dressings.

DIETARY INFORMATION:

May be used as written for general and high-fiber diets.
Low-cholesterol: Cut avocados to 1 pound 8 ounces and increase tomatoes to 4 pounds.

GUACAMOLE
(Southwestern)

YIELD: 1 gallon
PAN SIZE:

PORTION SIZE:
TEMPERATURE:

INGREDIENTS	WEIGHTS/MEASURES	FOR _____	METHOD
SPICY: Peeled and seeded avocados Seasoned salt Lemon pepper Finely minced onions Lemon juice Green food coloring Diced canned chiles QUICK AND EASY: Peeled and seeded avocados Seasoned salt Lemon juice	 1 ripened flat (size 24) ¼ cup 1 tablespoon 3 tablespoons 1⅓ cups ¼ teaspoon 1 4 ounce can 1 ripened flat (size 24) ¼ cup 1½ cups		1. Combine ingredients in mixer bowl. Mix at medium speed until well blended and shiny but coarse in texture with small bits of avocado. Allow flavors to combine for at least 30 minutes. May be stored, closely covered, in a refrigerator for up to 12 hours. 2. Use as a dip with toasted tortilla chips, as a salad on shredded lettuce, as a topping for tostados, taquitos, enchilados, burritos, chili rellenos, steaks and hamburgers, or as a spread for tortillas.

DIETARY INFORMATION:

May be used as written for general and high-fiber diets.
Low-cholesterol: May be used in small amounts as a garnish.

CELERY SLAW
(Florida)

YIELD: 50 portions (about 1½ gallons) **PORTION SIZE:** ½ cup
PAN SIZE: **TEMPERATURE:**

INGREDIENTS	WEIGHTS/MEASURES	FOR _____	METHOD
Sugar White vinegar Vegetable oil Salt White pepper Paprika Sour cream	¼ cup ½ cup 1⅓ cups 2 tablespoons ¼ teaspoon 2 teaspoons 2 cups		1. Beat sugar, vinegar, oil, salt, pepper, and paprika together until well blended. Add sour cream slowly while beating at low speed to form a dressing.
Thinly sliced celery Shredded raw carrots	1½ gallons 1 quart		2. Place celery and carrots in mixing bowl. Pour dressing over vegetables and toss lightly. Refrigerate until served. Toss lightly again just before serving. Drain any excess liquid from salad just before serving.

DIETARY INFORMATION:

May be used as written for general and high-fiber diets.
Diabetic: This recipe provides ½ bread and 1½ fat exchanges per portion.

COLE SLAW

YIELD: 50 portions (about 1½ gallons)
PAN SIZE:

PORTION SIZE: ½ cup
TEMPERATURE:

INGREDIENTS	WEIGHTS/MEASURES	FOR ____	METHOD
Cleaned, cored, and shredded cabbage Shredded carrots Chopped fresh green peppers Finely chopped onions Chopped parsley	6 pounds (about 3 gallons) 1½ quarts 1 cup 1 cup ¼ cup		1. Place cabbage in the bottom of a large mixing bowl. Add carrots, green peppers, onions, and parsley. Toss lightly.
Salad dressing Sugar Vinegar Celery seed Salt	3 cups 2 cups 1 cup 3 tablespoons 2½ tablespoons		2. Mix salad dressing, sugar, vinegar, celery seed, and salt together to form a dressing. 3. Pour dressing over vegetables. Mix lightly and refrigerate for 2 to 4 hours. Toss salad and dressing again just before it is served. Drain any excess liquid from salad just before serving.

DIETARY INFORMATION:
May be used as written for general, high-fiber, and bland diets.
Diabetic: This recipe provides 1 bread and 1 fat exchanges per portion.

NOTES:
Variation:
CARROT AND CABBAGE SLAW: Decrease cabbage to 4 pounds (about 2 gallons) and increase carrots to 5 pounds (about 1 gallon) in step 1.

MOLDED COLE SLAW

YIELD: 1 pan
PAN SIZE: 12 × 20 × 2-inch steam table pan

PORTION SIZE:
TEMPERATURE:

INGREDIENTS	WEIGHTS/MEASURES	FOR_____	METHOD
Lemon or lime flavored gelatin Hot water Salad dressing Vinegar Salt	1 pound 8 ounces 3 quarts 3 cups ¾ cup 1½ teaspoons		1. Dissolve gelatin in hot water. Cool to room temperature. 2. Combine salad dressing, vinegar, and salt. Add gelatin mixture gradually to dressing mixture while beating at low speed until smooth. Chill until thickened. Whip at high speed for 3 minutes or until fluffy.
Finely chopped cabbage Finely chopped green peppers Finely chopped onions Chopped pimientos Celery seed	2½ quarts 1 cup ½ cup ½ cup 1 tablespoon		3. Toss cabbage, green peppers, onions, pimientos, and celery seed together lightly to mix. Add to gelatin and pour into steam table pan. Chill until firm. 4. Cut into squares and serve chilled.

DIETARY INFORMATION:
May be used as written for general, high-fiber, and bland diets.

CRANBERRY RELISH
(New England)

YIELD: 1½ gallons
PAN SIZE:
PORTION SIZE:
TEMPERATURE:

INGREDIENTS	WEIGHTS/MEASURES	FOR _____	METHOD
Fresh cranberries Navel oranges Tart red apples Sugar	6 pounds 1 pound 2 pounds 2½ quarts		1. Wash cranberries. Remove any soft cranberries and any stems. Drain well. Grind coarsely into a large mixing bowl. 2. Wash oranges. Peel and keep orange peel. Remove and discard white membrane. Cut oranges into chunks, removing any seeds. Grind reserved orange peel and orange pulp coarsely and add to cranberries. 3. Wash and core apples. Remove any bruised or bad sections of the apples. Grind coarsely and add to cranberries and oranges. 4. Add sugar to cranberries, oranges, and apples. Mix lightly to blend. Refrigerate 24 hours before using.

DIETARY INFORMATION:

May be used as written for general, high-fiber, bland, low-cholesterol, and mild 2- to 3-gram sodium-restricted diets.

Diabetic: Use artificial sweetener instead of sugar. Up to 2 tablespoons may be served free.

CUCUMBER LETTUCE SALAD
(Midwestern)

YIELD: 50 portions (about 1½ gallons)   **PORTION SIZE:** ½ cup

PAN SIZE: **TEMPERATURE:**

INGREDIENTS	WEIGHTS/MEASURES	FOR ___	METHOD
Peeled and finely shredded cucumbers Finely chopped onions Salt	3 cups 1 cup ¼ cup		1. Squeeze as much liquid as possible from the cucumbers with the back of a spoon in a colander or china cap. Combine cucumbers with onions and salt. Cover and let set one-half hour. Rinse well with clear water. Drain well. Squeeze any excess liquid from cucumbers again.
White vinegar Sugar Chopped parsley Salad dressing or sour cream	½ cup 1 cup ¼ cup 1 cup		2. Combine vinegar, sugar, parsley, and salad dressing or sour cream. Combine cucumber mixture and dressing. Mix lightly and refrigerate until used.
Chopped lettuce Chopped parsley	1½ gallons (about 5 pounds) As necessary		3. Just before serving, toss lettuce with cucumber and dressing mixture. Garnish with chopped parsley and serve cold.

DIETARY INFORMATION:

May be used as written for general, high-fiber, and bland diets.
Diabetic: This recipe provides ½ fat exchange per portion.

FRIJOLE SALAD
(Southwestern)

YIELD: 50 portions (about 2¼ gallons) **PORTION SIZE:** ¾ cup
PAN SIZE: **TEMPERATURE:**

INGREDIENTS	WEIGHTS/MEASURES	FOR ____	METHOD
Canned rinsed and drained kidney beans	1½ quarts (one-half No. 10 can)		1. Combine beans and dressing. Cover and refrigerate 6 hours or overnight.
French dressing	1 quart		
Shredded cabbage	1¾ gallons (about 4 pounds)		2. Place cabbage in a large mixing bowl. Place tomatoes, cucumbers, and marinated beans on top. Toss lightly and serve.
Diced fresh tomatoes	2 quarts (about 2 pounds)		
Fresh pared peeled and thinly sliced cucumbers	1 quart (about 1 pound 8 ounces)		

DIETARY INFORMATION:

May be used as written for general, high-fiber, and bland diets.
Diabetic: This recipe provides 1 bread and 1½ fat exchanges per portion.

NOTES:
Variation:
FRIJOLE LETTUCE SALAD: Substitute 1¾ gallons shredded lettuce for cabbage in step 2. Add 3 cups sliced sweet onions or green onions and tops. Toss lightly and serve.

WILTED LETTUCE
(Midwestern and Pennsylvania Dutch)

YIELD: 50 portions (about 1 gallon) **PORTION SIZE:** 1/3 cup
PAN SIZE: **TEMPERATURE:**

INGREDIENTS	WEIGHTS/MEASURES	FOR____	METHOD
Head lettuce	4 pounds		1. Clean lettuce. Cut or tear into about 1-inch cubes. Place lettuce in large mixing bowl.
Chopped bacon All purpose flour Sugar Salt	8 ounces 1/3 cup 1/2 cup 1 tablespoon		2. Fry bacon over low heat in heavy frying pan, stirring occasionally, until bacon is crisp. Stir flour, sugar, and salt into hot bacon and fat. Mix until smooth.
Water Vinegar	2 cups 1 cup		3. Combine water and vinegar. Add gradually to hot bacon mixture. Cook, stirring constantly, over moderate heat until thickened. 4. Pour hot sauce over lettuce. Toss lightly and serve warm.

DIETARY INFORMATION:

May be used as written for general, high-fiber, and bland diets.
Diabetic: This recipe provides 1/2 fat and 1/2 bread exchanges per portion.

LIMA BEAN SALAD

YIELD: 50 portions (about 1½ gallons)
PAN SIZE:

PORTION SIZE: ½ cup
TEMPERATURE:

INGREDIENTS	WEIGHTS/MEASURES	FOR _____	METHOD
Frozen baby lima beans	5 pounds		1. Cook beans as directed on the package. Cool to lukewarm.
Chopped celery Finely chopped onions Chopped fresh green peppers Chopped pimientos	1½ quarts 2 cups 2 cups ½ cup		2. Add celery, onions, green peppers, and pimientos to beans. Toss lightly.
Sour cream Salad dressing Salt Chopped parsley	2 cups 2 cups 1 tablespoon As necessary		3. Combine sour cream, salad dressing, and salt. Mix to blend. Add to salad and toss lightly to blend. Refrigerate until served. Serve cold garnished with parsley.

DIETARY INFORMATION:

May be used as written for general, high-fiber, and bland diets.
Diabetic: This recipe provides 1 fat and 1 bread exchanges per portion.
Low-cholesterol: Use 1 quart vinegar and oil dressing instead of dressing ingredients in step 3.

MACARONI SLAW
(Midwestern)

YIELD: 50 portions (about 1½ gallons) **PORTION SIZE:** ½ cup
PAN SIZE: **TEMPERATURE:**

INGREDIENTS	WEIGHTS/MEASURES	FOR ____	METHOD
Shell macaroni Boiling water Salt Vegetable oil	1½ quarts (1 pound 8 ounces) 1½ gallons 1 tablespoon 2 tablespoons		1. Stir macaroni into boiling salted water. Add oil. Stir to mix well. Cook 10 minutes or until tender, stirring occasionally. Rinse with cold water. Drain well. Place in mixing bowl and stir to separate.
Shredded cabbage Shredded carrots Finely chopped fresh green peppers Finely chopped onions	2½ quarts 3 cups 1½ cups 1½ cups		2. Add cabbage, carrots, green peppers, and onions to macaroni. Mix lightly.
Salad dressing Lemon juice Sugar Prepared mustard Salt Garlic powder	3 cups ½ cup 3 tablespoons 2 tablespoons 1 tablespoon ½ teaspoon		3. Mix salad dressing, lemon juice, sugar, mustard, salt, and garlic powder to blend. Pour over salad. Mix lightly to coat vegetables and macaroni with dressing. Refrigerate until served.

DIETARY INFORMATION:

May be used as written for general and high-fiber diets.
Diabetic: This recipe provides 1 bread and 1 fat exchanges per portion.

GRATED POTATO SALAD
(Midwestern)

YIELD: 50 portions (about 1½ gallons)   **PORTION SIZE:** ½ cup

PAN SIZE: **TEMPERATURE:**

INGREDIENTS	WEIGHTS/MEASURES	FOR ___	METHOD
Red potatoes	12 pounds		1. Cover potatoes with boiling water. Cook until tender. Cool and peel. Grate potatoes coarsely when they are cool enough to handle.
Salad dressing Finely chopped celery Hard cooked eggs Finely chopped pimiento Finely chopped onions Salad mustard Salt Drained sweet pickle relish	1½ quarts 3 cups 16 ½ cup 1½ cups ¼ cup 2 tablespoons 1 cup		2. Combine dressing, celery, eggs, pimiento, onions, mustard, salt, and pickle relish in a large mixing bowl. Mix to blend well. Add grated potatoes and stir lightly until potatoes and dressing are well mixed. Refrigerate until served.

DIETARY INFORMATION:
May be used as written for general and bland diets.

SAUERKRAUT SALAD

YIELD: 1 gallon
PAN SIZE:

PORTION SIZE:
TEMPERATURE:

INGREDIENTS	WEIGHTS/MEASURES	FOR ___	METHOD
Drained and chopped sauerkraut	3 quarts (1 No. 10 can)		1. Place kraut, celery, green peppers, carrots, and onions in mixing bowl. Toss lightly.
Thinly sliced celery	2 cups		
Diced fresh green peppers	2 cups		
Grated carrots	2 cups		
Finely chopped onions	2 cups		
Sugar	1 quart		2. Mix sugar, juice, vinegar, and salad oil together. Add to kraut and vegetables. Toss to coat all of vegetables and kraut with dressing. Refrigerate at least 4 hours and preferably overnight.
Juice drained from peaches canned in heavy syrup	2¼ cups		
Vinegar	2 cups		
Salad oil	1½ cups		3. Drain well before serving.

DIETARY INFORMATION:
May be used as written for general, high-fiber, low-cholesterol, and bland diets.

NOTES: This recipe was developed by Beatrice Eskew of Gainesville, Missouri.

MOLDED STRAWBERRIES AND CREAM CHEESE
(Midwestern)

YIELD: 1 pan

PAN SIZE: 12 × 20 × 2-inch steam table pan

PORTION SIZE:

TEMPERATURE:

INGREDIENTS	WEIGHTS/MEASURES	FOR _____	METHOD
Strawberry flavored gelatin Sugar Hot water	1 pound 8 ounces 2 cups 3½ quarts		1. Dissolve gelatin and sugar in hot water.
Fresh strawberries Softened cream cheese Whipped topping (optional)	2 quarts 3 cups (1 pound 8 ounces) 2 quarts		2. Wash, hull, and slice strawberries. Add to gelatin. 3. Reserve 1½ quarts of gelatin and fruit. Pour remaining gelatin into a steam table pan. Chill until set but not quite firm. 4. Chill reserved gelatin and strawberries until slightly thickened. Add cream cheese gradually while beating at low speed blending well. Pour over clear fruited gelatin and chill until firm. 5. Cut into squares and serve with whipped topping if desired.

DIETARY INFORMATION:

May be used as written for general, bland, and mild 2- to 3-gram sodium-restricted diets.

SALAD DRESSING FOR VEGETABLES

YIELD: 1 gallon
PAN SIZE:
PORTION SIZE:
TEMPERATURE:

INGREDIENTS	WEIGHTS/MEASURES	FOR _____	METHOD
Tomato catsup	3 cups		1. Beat catsup, vinegar, water, paprika, oil, and sugar together at medium speed for 2 minutes. Let set one-half hour and then beat again for 2 minutes. Cover and refrigerate until needed.
Cider vinegar	3 cups		
Water	1 cup		
Paprika	1½ tablespoons		
Vegetable oil	2 quarts		2. Mix well before serving.
Sugar	1¾ cups		

DIETARY INFORMATION:

May be used as written for general, low-cholesterol, bland, and soft diets.

Vegetables

Escalloped Apples 143
Baked Beans (Midwestern) 144
Boston Baked Beans (New England) 145
Red Beans and Rice (Southern) 146
Refried Beans (Southwestern) 147
    Plain Refried Beans 147
Cabbage with Hot Vinegar Dressing (Pennsylvania Dutch) 148
Spicy Cabbage 149
Deep Fried Corn on the Cob 150
Simmered Greens (Southern) 151
Fried Okra (Southern) 152
Black-Eyed Peas with Rice (Southern) 153
Escalloped Potatoes 154
Mashed Potatoes 155
    Hot Potato Salad 155
Sauerkraut with Tomatoes 156
Pineapple Glazed Yams 157
    Spicy Pineapple Glazed Yams 157
Raisin Glazed Yams 158
Zucchini in Creole Sauce (Louisiana) 159
Guidelines for Cooking Fresh Vegetables 160
Guidelines for Cooking Frozen Vegetables 161

Information

In many parts of the world, the first appearance of fresh vegetables in the spring is a cause for celebration. The seasons are not as important now that modern processing and transportation have made them available throughout the year. However, the corn and strawberry festivals in our country show that people still enjoy celebrating the bounty of the land. Vegetables have always been important in the diet of most cultures, and now that research is showing the value of their fiber content, it is particularly important to include them in menus. Many menu planners say patrons and residents won't eat vegetables, but it has been proven that most people will eat vegetables if they are well prepared and served attractively.

It is a good idea to feature vegetables on menus during the season when they are most abundant, but unless they are truly fresh it is often better to use frozen or canned vegetables which are packed and processed at the peak of their flavor and vitamin content.

Guidelines for Using Fresh Vegetables.

1. Vegetables should be clean and most vegetables should be washed well, even if they are peeled before they are used.
2. Vegetables should be cut into uniform, manageable pieces. They should not be too large to handle nor should they be cut so small that they lose their identity (except for special diets).
3. Vegetables should not be soaked in water a long time before they are prepared. Long soaking will remove some of the vitamins from vegetables.
4. Vegetables should be handled carefully before and after cooking to prevent breaking and give them a more attractive appearance.
5. Vegetables should always be prepared as close to serving time as possible. If served over a period of time, the vegetables should be prepared in batches.
6. Vegetables should generally be cooked in as small an amount of boiling water as possible, except for a few strong vegetables where the recipe includes instructions for the use of more water.
7. Vegetables should be cooked in boiling water. Vegetables should not be put in cold water and the water brought to a boil unless the recipe includes those specific instructions.
8. Vegetables should never be overcooked. Instructions for cooking times should be followed closely.
9. Vegetable juices, except for some strong-flavored ones, should be saved and used in gravies and soups. The use of vegetable juices will improve both the flavor and nutritive value of gravies and soups.
10. Baking soda should never be added to vegetables because it destroys the vitamins they contain.

Guidelines for Using Canned Vegetables.

1. Food from a can which bulges, leaks, is dented at the seams, or has liquid which is milky, off color, or foamy should not be used.
2. Canned vegetables should be simmered in their own juice 10 to 12 minutes except for beets and spinach, which should be simmered 20 minutes in order to kill any harmful bacteria which might be in the canned foods.
3. A Number 10 can of food will generally yield 25 $\frac{1}{2}$-cup portions.
4. Canned vegetables should be heated as close as possible to serving time.
5. After canned vegetables are heated, they should be drained and put into serving pans. Add $\frac{1}{2}$ cup (1 stick) butter or margarine for each Number 10 can of vegetable used.
6. Leftover vegetables should be covered and refrigerated as soon as possible.

ESCALLOPED APPLES

YIELD: 50 portions (about 1½ gallons)
PAN SIZE: Roaster
PORTION SIZE: ½ cup
TEMPERATURE: 350°F Oven

INGREDIENTS	WEIGHTS/MEASURES	FOR ____	METHOD
Brown sugar Salt Ground cinnamon Ground cloves	2 cups 1 teaspoon 1 teaspoon 1 teaspoon		1. Combine brown sugar, salt, cinnamon, and cloves. Mix well and set aside for use in steps 3 and 4.
Firm tart apples	12 pounds 8 ounces		2. Wash and core apples. Cut into wedges. Spread one-half of the wedges evenly over the bottom of a well-buttered roaster.
Coarsely crushed white soda crackers Melted butter or margarine Hot water or fruit juice	2 quarts (1 pound) 1½ cups (3 sticks) 2 quarts		3. Spread crackers evenly over apples and then sprinkle evenly with one-half of the sugar mixture. 4. Pour melted fat and hot water or fruit juice evenly over the apples and crackers. Spread with remaining apples. Sprinkle with remaining sugar mixture. 5. Bake 45 minutes or until apples are tender. Serve hot.

DIETARY INFORMATION:
May be used as written for general, bland, and soft diets.
Low-cholesterol: Use margarine in step 4.

NOTES: This recipe is not very sweet because it is generally served with the main course and not as a dessert.

BAKED BEANS
(Midwestern)

YIELD: 50 portions (about 3 gallons)
PAN SIZE: Roaster
PORTION SIZE: 1 cup
TEMPERATURE: 325°F Oven

INGREDIENTS	WEIGHTS/MEASURES	FOR _____	METHOD
Dry navy or great northern beans Cold water	8 pounds (4⅔ quarts) 1½ gallons		1. Pick over beans. Remove any dark or discolored beans. Wash thoroughly with cold water. Drain well. Cover with cold water and bring to a boil. Boil 2 minutes. Remove from heat. 2. Cover beans and let stand 1 to 2 hours.
Canned crushed tomatoes Salt Hot water	3 quarts (1 No. 10 can) ¼ cup As necessary		3. Bring beans and the water in which they were soaked to a boil. Add tomatoes and salt. Cover and simmer 1½ hours or until beans are tender but not mushy. Add additional hot water, if necessary, to keep beans covered with liquid while simmering.
Chopped bacon Coarsely chopped onions Brown sugar Dark corn syrup Prepared mustard Tomato catsup	2 pounds 2 quarts 3 cups 3 cups 1 cup 2 cups		4. Combine bacon, onions, brown sugar, syrup, mustard, and catsup. Mix well and add to beans. Mix well. 5. Place beans in roasting pan. Cover tightly and bake 3 hours. Remove cover and bake another 30 minutes.

DIETARY INFORMATION:

May be used as written for general, high-fiber, and bland diets.
Low-cholesterol: Delete bacon and add 1 pound margarine in step 4.

BOSTON BAKED BEANS
(New England)

YIELD: 50 portions (about 3 gallons)　　**PORTION SIZE:** 1 cup
PAN SIZE: Roaster　　**TEMPERATURE:** 350°F Oven

INGREDIENTS	WEIGHTS/MEASURES	FOR ____	METHOD
Dry great northern or pea beans Cold water	8 pounds (4 2/3 quarts) 2 1/2 gallons		1. Pick over beans. Remove any dark or discolored beans. Wash thoroughly with cold water. Drain well. Cover with cold water and bring to a boil. Boil 2 minutes. Remove from heat. 2. Cover beans and let stand 1 to 2 hours.
Hot water	As necessary		3. Bring beans and water in which they were soaked to a boil. Add hot water, if necessary, to cover beans. Cover and simmer 1 1/2 hours or until beans are tender but not mushy.
Chopped onions Salt Brown sugar Molasses Vinegar Ground mustard Ground cloves Salt pork with rind removed and cut into 1/2-inch pieces Hot water	1 quart 1/4 cup 2 1/2 cups 2 cups 1/4 cup 1/4 cup 1 teaspoon 2 pounds As necessary		4. Add onions, salt, brown sugar, molasses, vinegar, mustard, cloves, and salt pork to beans. Mix thoroughly and place in roaster. 5. Cover roaster and bake 3 to 4 hours. Add extra hot water, if necessary, to keep beans just covered with juice the first 3 hours. Remove the cover the last hour to allow beans to brown. Stir beans once during the last hour to mix the brown top into the beans.

DIETARY INFORMATION:

May be used as written for general, high-fiber, and bland diets.
Low-cholesterol: Delete salt pork and add 1 pound margarine in step 4.

RED BEANS AND RICE
(Southern)

YIELD: 50 portions (about 1½ gallons each of rice and beans)
PAN SIZE: Heavy 3-gallon stockpot
PORTION SIZE: ½ cup each rice and beans
TEMPERATURE:

INGREDIENTS	WEIGHTS/MEASURES	FOR _____	METHOD
Chopped bacon Chopped onions	1 pound 8 ounces 3 cups		1. Fry bacon and onions together in stockpot over moderate heat, stirring frequently, until onions are lightly browned. Do not drain.
Undrained canned kidney beans Pepper Hot sauce	1½ gallons (2 No. 10 cans) 1 teaspoon 1 teaspoon		2. Add beans with juice, pepper, and hot sauce to bacon and onions. Cover and simmer over low heat for 20 minutes, stirring occasionally.
Long-grain rice Cold water Salt Vegetable oil	2 pounds 12 ounces (about 1½ quarts) 3 quarts 3 tablespoons 2 tablespoons		3. Combine rice, cold water, salt, and vegetable oil in stockpot. Bring to a boil, stirring occasionally. Cover tightly. Simmer 15 minutes without stirring. If rice is not tender, cover and simmer another 2 to 3 minutes. 4. Uncover rice. Allow it to dry and fluff for 3 to 5 minutes. 5. Serve ½ cup hot bean mixture over ½ cup hot rice.

DIETARY INFORMATION:

May be used as written for general and high-fiber diets.
Low-cholesterol: Brown onions in 3 cups margarine or vegetable oil instead of bacon in step 1.

REFRIED BEANS
(Southwestern)

YIELD: 50 portions (about 1½ gallons)
PAN SIZE: Heavy 3-gallon stockpot
12 × 20 × 2-inch steam table pan

PORTION SIZE: ½ cup each
TEMPERATURE: 350°F Oven

INGREDIENTS	WEIGHTS/MEASURES	FOR ___	METHOD
Dry pinto beans Water	4 pounds (about 2½ quarts) As necessary		1. Pick over beans. Wash thoroughly in cold water. Remove any dark or discolored beans. Cover with water and bring to a boil. Boil 2 minutes. Set aside for 1½ to 2 hours.
Salt Pepper Water	2 tablespoons 1½ teaspoons As necessary		2. Add salt, pepper, and enough water to cover the beans. Cover and simmer 1½ hours or until beans are tender but not mushy. Add boiling water if beans become dry.
Chili powder Dehydrated garlic	¾ cup 2½ tablespoons		3. Add chili powder and garlic to beans. Cook an additional hour adding more hot water if necessary to keep beans from burning. Drain well reserving bean stock for use in step 5. 4. Place beans in mixer bowl. Beat at low speed until beans are mashed.
Shredded cheddar cheese Chopped onions Hot sauce Hot bean stock	1 pound 8 ounces (1½ quarts) 1½ cups 1 tablespoon As necessary		5. Add 1 quart shredded cheese, onions, 3 cups hot bean stock and hot sauce to beans. Beat at medium speed adding more bean stock if necessary to get the consistency of mashed potatoes. 6. Spread bean mixture in greased steam table pan. 7. Bake 30 minutes. Sprinkle remaining shredded cheese over beans and serve hot.

DIETARY INFORMATION:

May be used as written for general and high-fiber diets for those accustomed to highly spiced foods.
Diabetic: This recipe provides 1½ bread, 1½ meat, and 1 fat exchanges per portion.
This recipe provides 1½ ounces protein per portion.

NOTES:
Variation:
PLAIN REFRIED BEANS: Omit chili powder, garlic, cheese, onions, and hot sauce. Mashed bean mixture may be fried in heavy frying pan over low heat in shortening or bacon fat until browned around the edges.

CABBAGE WITH HOT VINEGAR DRESSING
(Pennsylvania Dutch)

YIELD: 50 portions (about 1½ gallons)
PAN SIZE: Heavy 3-gallon stockpot
PORTION SIZE: ½ cup
TEMPERATURE:

INGREDIENTS	WEIGHTS/MEASURES	FOR ___	METHOD
Fresh white cabbage Salt Boiling water	11 pounds 1 tablespoon 2 quarts		1. Trim and wash cabbage. Shred coarsely and add to boiling water. Cover tightly and cook in steam for 12 minutes. Drain well.
Diced bacon Vinegar Sugar Salt Pepper	1 pound 3 cups ½ cup 1 tablespoon ¼ teaspoon		2. Cook bacon in heavy frying pan over low heat, stirring occasionally, until crisp. Do not drain. 3. Stir vinegar, sugar, salt, and pepper into bacon and bacon fat. Heat over moderate heat, stirring constantly, till mixture boils. Pour hot sauce over hot cabbage. Mix lightly and serve hot.

DIETARY INFORMATION:

May be used as written for general and high-fiber diets.

Diabetic: This recipe provides 1 fat and ½ bread exchanges per portion.

Low-cholesterol: Substitute 2 cups (1 pound) margarine for bacon and bacon fat and increase salt to 1½ tablespoons in step 2.

SPICY CABBAGE

YIELD: 50 portions (about 1½ gallons)
PAN SIZE: Heavy 3-gallon stockpot
PORTION SIZE: ½ cup
TEMPERATURE:

INGREDIENTS	WEIGHTS/MEASURES	FOR_____	METHOD
Chopped bacon	8 ounces		1. Fry bacon over low heat, stirring occasionally, in stockpot. Do not drain.
Tomato juice Beef bouillon Garlic powder Powdered oregano Salt Pepper	1 quart 1 quart 1½ teaspoons 1½ teaspoons 1 tablespoon ¼ teaspoon		2. Add tomato juice, bouillon, garlic, oregano, salt, and pepper to bacon. Cover tightly and simmer 5 minutes.
Fresh white cabbage	12 pounds 8 ounces		3. Trim and wash cabbage. Shred coarsely and add to boiling sauce. Cover tightly and cook over medium heat for 12 minutes, stirring occasionally. Serve hot.

DIETARY INFORMATION:

May be used as written for general and high-fiber diets.
Diabetic: This recipe provides ½ fat and ½ bread exchanges per portion.
Low-cholesterol: Use ½ cup margarine instead of bacon in step 1.

DEEP FRIED CORN ON THE COB

YIELD: 50 portions
PAN SIZE:

PORTION SIZE: 1 ear
TEMPERATURE: 300°F Deep fat

INGREDIENTS	WEIGHTS/MEASURES	FOR _____	METHOD
Fresh corn on the cob	50 ears (about 18 pounds)		1. Clean corn. Wash thoroughly. Drain and dry thoroughly.
Plain or seasoned salt	As necessary		2. Fry 3 minutes. Drain well in basket or on absorbent paper. Do not let kernels brown during cooking.
			3. Serve hot with plain or seasoned salt.

DIETARY INFORMATION:

May be used as written for general or high-fiber diets.
May be used for mild 2- to 3-gram sodium-restricted diets if salt substitute is used.
Diabetic: This recipe provides 1 bread and ½ fat exchanges per 4-inch ear of corn.
Low-cholesterol: Deep-fat fry corn in vegetable oil.

SIMMERED GREENS
(Southern)

YIELD: 50 portions (about 1½ gallons)
PAN SIZE: Heavy 3-gallon stockpot
PORTION SIZE: ½ cup
TEMPERATURE:

INGREDIENTS	WEIGHTS/MEASURES	FOR_____	METHOD
Boiling water Chopped bacon	1 gallon 1 pound		1. Combine water and bacon in stockpot. Cover and simmer 30 minutes.
Frozen collard, mustard, or turnip greens Salt Pepper	10 pounds 2 tablespoons ¾ teaspoon		2. Add greens, salt, and pepper to water. Cover and simmer 1½ hours. 3. Cut through greens several times before serving hot with juice (pot liquor).

DIETARY INFORMATION:

May be used as written for general and high-fiber diets.
Diabetic: This recipe provides ⅓ fat exchange per portion.

FRIED OKRA
(Southern)

YIELD: 50 portions (about 1¼ gallons)
PAN SIZE:
PORTION SIZE: ⅓ cup
TEMPERATURE: 375°F Griddle

INGREDIENTS	WEIGHTS/MEASURES	FOR _____	METHOD
Frozen okra Cornmeal All-purpose flour Salt Pepper	7 pounds 8 ounces 3 cups 2 cups 1½ tablespoons 1 teaspoon		1. Thaw okra and cut into 1-inch pieces. Dredge in a mixture of the cornmeal, flour, salt, and pepper.
Shortening	2 cups		2. Fry okra on well-greased griddle or in heavy frying pan for about 10 minutes or until golden brown. 3. Serve hot.

DIETARY INFORMATION:

May be used as written for general and high-fiber diets.
Low-cholesterol: Use vegetable oil instead of shortening for frying okra in step 2.

BLACK-EYED PEAS WITH RICE
(Southern)

YIELD: 50 portions (about 2¼ gallons)   **PORTION SIZE:** ⅔ cup
PAN SIZE: Heavy 3-gallon stockpot   **TEMPERATURE:**

INGREDIENTS	WEIGHTS/MEASURES	FOR ___	METHOD
Chopped bacon Chopped onions	12 ounces 3 cups		1. Fry bacon and onions together in heavy stockpot over moderate heat, stirring frequently, until lightly browned. Do not drain.
Long-grain rice	3 pounds (about 1¾ quarts)		2. Add rice to bacon. Cook and stir over moderate heat for 2 minutes.
Undrained canned black-eyed peas Hot water Black pepper Hot sauce	1¾ quarts (4 No. 300 cans) 3½ quarts 1 teaspoon 1 teaspoon		3. Add black-eyed peas, water, pepper, and hot sauce to rice. Stir to mix. Cover tightly and simmer 20 minutes or until rice is tender. Serve hot.

DIETARY INFORMATION:

May be used as written for general and high-fiber diets.
Low-cholesrerol: Delete bacon and fry onions in 1½ cups margarine in step 1.

ESCALLOPED POTATOES

YIELD: 50 portions (2 pans)
PAN SIZE: Heavy 5-gallon stockpot
12 × 20 × 2-inch steam table pans

PORTION SIZE: ½ cup
TEMPERATURE: 350°F Oven

INGREDIENTS	WEIGHTS/MEASURES	FOR ___	METHOD
Sliced peeled fresh white potatoes Boiling water Salt	12 pounds 8 ounces As necessary 1 tablespoon		1. Place potatoes in stockpot. Cover with boiling water and salt. Bring to a boil and cook about 10 minutes or until barely tender. Drain well. Put one half of the potatoes in each of 2 well-buttered pans.
Butter or margarine All-purpose flour Salt Pepper Nonfat dry milk Hot water Paprika	1½ cups (3 sticks) 1½ cups 1½ tablespoons ½ teaspoon 2 quarts 1¼ gallons 2 teaspoons		2. Cook and stir butter or margarine, flour, salt, and pepper together in a saucepan over low heat until smooth but not browned to form a roux. Remove from heat. 3. Stir dry milk into hot water. Return roux to heat and add hot milk all at once. Cook and stir over moderate heat using a wire whip until sauce is smooth and thickened. 4. Pour half of the sauce over the potatoes in each pan. Stir lightly to mix sauce and potatoes. Sprinkle lightly with paprika. 5. Bake 1 hour or until lightly browned and bubbling. Serve hot.

DIETARY INFORMATION:
May be used as written for general, soft, and mild 2- to 3-gram sodium-restricted diets.
Diabetic: This recipe provides 1 bread and 1½ fat exchanges per portion.
Low-cholesterol: Use margarine instead of butter in step 2.

NOTES:
1. Fourteen pounds 8 ounces of fresh white potatoes will yield approximately 12 pounds 8 ounces of peeled potatoes.
2. Two pounds of dehydrated sliced white potatoes can be cooked according to the directions on the container and used instead of the fresh potatoes in step 1.

MASHED POTATOES

YIELD: 50 portions (about 1½ gallons)
PAN SIZE: Heavy 5-gallon stockpot
PORTION SIZE: ½ cup (No. 8 dipper)
TEMPERATURE:

INGREDIENTS	WEIGHTS/MEASURES	FOR _____	METHOD
Peeled and quartered fresh white potatoes Boiling water Salt	12 pounds 8 ounces As necessary 2 tablespoons		1. Place potatoes in stockpot. Cover with boiling water and salt. Bring to a boil. Reduce heat and simmer 20 to 25 minutes or until tender. Drain well. Place potatoes in mixer bowl and beat at low speed until broken up.
Salt Butter or margarine	2 tablespoons 1 cup (2 sticks)		2. Add salt and butter or margarine to potatoes. Beat at high speed 3 to 5 minutes or until smooth and fluffy.
Nonfat dry milk Warm water	1½ cups 2 cups		3. Stir milk into warm water and add to potatoes. Beat another 2 minutes or until light and fluffy. Serve hot.

DIETARY INFORMATION:

May be used as written for general, bland, and soft diets.
Diabetic: This recipe provides 1 bread and ½ fat exchanges per portion.
Low-cholesterol: Use margarine instead of butter in step 2.

NOTES: Fourteen pounds 8 ounces of fresh white potatoes will yield approximately 12 pounds 8 ounces of peeled potatoes.

Variation:
HOT POTATO SALAD: Use 1 cup of water in step 3. Add 2 cups salad dressing, 1½ cups finely chopped onions, 10 chopped hard-cooked eggs, 1 cup finely chopped fresh green peppers, 1 tablespoon salad mustard, and ½ cup finely chopped pimientos to mashed potatoes after step 3. Serve warm.

SAUERKRAUT WITH TOMATOES

YIELD: 50 portions (about 1½ gallons)
PAN SIZE: Heavy 3-gallon stockpot
　　　　　　　Roaster
PORTION SIZE: ½ cup
TEMPERATURE: 350°F

INGREDIENTS	WEIGHTS/MEASURES	FOR_____	METHOD
Chopped onions Vegetable oil	1 quart 1 cup		1. Fry onions in stockpot over low heat in vegetable oil, stirring occasionally, until onions are transparent.
Canned crushed Italian-style tomatoes Hot fat-free chicken broth Sugar Ground cloves Thyme Pepper Salt	3 quarts (1 No. 10 can) 2 quarts 1 cup 1 teaspoon 2 teaspoons 1 teaspoon 1 teaspoon		2. Add tomatoes, broth, sugar, cloves, thyme, pepper, and salt to the onions. Simmer 5 minutes over low heat.
Well-drained sauerkraut	1½ gallons (2 No. 10 cans)		3. Add sauerkraut to tomato sauce. Mix well. Place in roasting pan. Cover tightly and bake 2 hours. Serve hot.

DIETARY INFORMATION:
May be used as written for general, high-fiber, and low-cholesterol diets.
Diabetic: This recipe provides 1 bread and 1 fat exchanges per portion.

PINEAPPLE GLAZED YAMS

YIELD: 48 portions (2 pans)
PAN SIZE: 12 × 20 × 2-inch steam table pans
PORTION SIZE: ½ cup
TEMPERATURE: 350°F Oven

INGREDIENTS	WEIGHTS/MEASURES	FOR ____	METHOD
Canned yams	1½ gallons (2 No. 10 cans)		1. Drain yams well. Discard juice. Place one half of the yams in each steam table pan which has been greased heavily with margarine.
Margarine	½ cup (1 stick)		
Drained crushed pineapple	3 quarts (1 No. 10 can)		2. Combine pineapple, brown sugar, margarine, and salt in mixer bowl. Mix 1 minute at low speed or until blended. Spread one half of the pineapple mixture evenly over the yams in each pan.
Brown sugar	1 quart		3. Cover with aluminum foil and bake 30 minutes. Remove foil and bake another 30 minutes or until lightly browned.
Margarine	2 cups (4 sticks)		
Salt	2 teaspoons		

DIETARY INFORMATION:

May be used as written for general, high-fiber, low-cholesterol, bland, soft, and mild 2- to 3-gram sodium-restricted diets.

NOTES:

Variation:
SPICY PINEAPPLE GLAZED YAMS: Add 2 tablespoons of pumpkin pie spice in step 2.

RAISIN GLAZED YAMS

YIELD: 48 portions (2 pans)
PAN SIZE: 12 × 20 × 2-inch steam table pans
PORTION SIZE: ½ cup
TEMPERATURE: 375°F Oven

INGREDIENTS	WEIGHTS/MEASURES	FOR ___	METHOD
Yams canned in heavy syrup Margarine	1½ gallons (2 No. 10 cans) ½ cup (1 stick)		1. Drain yams. Keep juice for use in step 2. Place one half of the yams evenly in each steam table pan which has been greased heavily with margarine.
Brown sugar Margarine Syrup from yams Raisins Salt	2 cups 1 cup (2 sticks) 3 cups 3 cups 2 teaspoons		2. Combine brown sugar, margarine, syrup, raisins, and salt. Cook and stir over moderate heat until sugar is dissolved. Cook 1 minute longer and then pour one half of the hot syrup over yams in each pan. 3. Cover with aluminum foil and bake 15 minutes. Remove foil and bake another 15 minutes or until lightly browned and glazed. Baste with pan juice during the last 15 minutes.

DIETARY INFORMATION:
May be used as written for general, high-fiber, low-cholesterol, bland, and mild 2- to 3-gram sodium-restricted diets.

ZUCCHINI IN CREOLE SAUCE
(Louisiana)

YIELD: 50 portions (about 1½ gallons)
PAN SIZE: Heavy 3-gallon stockpot
PORTION SIZE: ½ cup
TEMPERATURE:

INGREDIENTS	WEIGHTS/MEASURES	FOR ____	METHOD
Chopped bacon Chopped celery Chopped onions Chopped fresh green peppers	1 pound 1 quart 1 quart 1 quart		1. Fry bacon over low heat in heavy stockpot, stirring occasionally, until bacon is crisp. Add celery, onions, and green peppers. Cook, stirring occasionally, over low heat until onions are golden.
Tomato sauce Ground oregano Garlic powder Pepper Salt	1 quart 1 tablespoon 2 teaspoons ¼ teaspoon 1½ tablespoons		2. Add tomato sauce, oregano, garlic, pepper, and salt to vegetables. Cover and cook over moderate heat, stirring occasionally, for 10 minutes.
Fresh zucchini OR Frozen zucchini Chopped fresh parsley	12 pounds 10 pounds About ½ cup		3. Wash fresh zucchini, remove both ends and slice into about ¼-inch rounds. Add to tomato sauce. Cook, stirring occasionally, over moderate heat about 10 minutes or until zucchini is tender. Do not overcook. Serve hot garnished with chopped parsley.

DIETARY INFORMATION:
May be used as written for general and high-fiber diets.
Diabetic: This recipe provides ½ bread and 1½ fat exchanges per portion.
Low-cholesterol: Substitute 2 cups (1 pound) margarine for bacon and bacon fat in step 1.

GUIDELINES FOR COOKING FRESH VEGETABLES

YIELD: 25 portions (about 3 quarts)　　　　　　　　　　　　　　　　　　　　　**EACH PORTION:** 1/2 cup (3 to 4 ounces)

Vegetable	Amount to Buy	Approximate Amount of Water to Use	Approximate Time to Cook	Method
Asparagus	9 pounds	1 1/2 quarts	10 to 20 minutes	1. Bring the water to a boil in a heavy stockpot or steam-jacketed kettle.
Green or wax beans	6 pounds	2 quarts	20 to 30 minutes	
Beets	7 pounds	To cover	60 to 90 minutes	2. Add 1 teaspoon salt for each quart of water.
Broccoli	7 pounds	3 quarts	10 to 12 minutes	
Brussels sprouts	7 pounds	3 quarts	10 to 15 minutes	3. Add vegetables and bring water back to a boil. Cook until vegetables are just tender.
Cabbage	6 pounds, 8 ounces	3 quarts	10 to 12 minutes	
Carrots	6 pounds, 8 ounces	2 quarts	15 to 20 minutes	4. Drain vegetables; save juice for use in soups, sauces, and gravies. Add butter or margarine, if desired, and serve hot.
Cauliflower	12 pounds, 8 ounces	3 quarts	12 minutes	
Corn on the cob	12 pounds, 12 ounces	To cover	16 minutes	
Eggplant	7 pounds	To cover	5 to 10 minutes	
Greens	7 pounds	1 quart	20 to 30 minutes	
Onions	5 pounds, 8 ounces	3 quarts	15 to 20 minutes	
Parsnips	6 pounds	To cover	20 minutes	
Sweet potatoes	8 pounds	To cover	25 to 35 minutes	
White potatoes	8 pounds	To cover	20 to 25 minutes	
Summer squash	6 pounds	1 cup	20 minutes	
Turnips	6 pounds	2 quarts	20 to 30 minutes	

Notes:
1. Peel and prepare vegetables as close to serving time as possible.
2. Cooking times for fresh vegetables will vary according to the age and tenderness of the vegetables.
3. Cook vegetables in small quantities and as near to serving time as possible.
4. Any leftover vegetables should be covered and refrigerated as soon as possible.

GUIDELINES FOR COOKING FROZEN VEGETABLES

YIELD: 50 portions (about 1 1/2 gallons)   **EACH PORTION:** 1/2 cup (3 to 4 ounces)

Vegetable	Weight	Approximate Amount of Water to Use	Approximate Time to Cook	Method
Asparagus	10 pounds	3 quarts	8 to 10 minutes	1. Tap frozen vegetables in package lightly to break up blocks.
Green or wax beans	10 pounds	1 gallon	10 to 15 minutes	2. Bring water to a boil in a stockpot or steam-jacketed kettle.
French style green beans	10 pounds	3 quarts	6 to 8 minutes	3. Add 1 teaspoon salt for each quart of water.
Lima beans	10 pounds	1 gallon	12 to 14 minutes	4. Add vegetables; bring the water back to a boil.
Broccoli	10 pounds	1 gallon	7 to 9 minutes	5. Reduce heat and cook, uncovered, until vegetables are just tender. Lima beans, cauliflower, corn, succotash, and summer squash are cooked covered.
Brussels sprouts	10 pounds	3 1/2 quarts	7 to 10 minutes	6. Drain vegetables; save liquid for use in soups, sauces, and gravies. Add butter or margarine, if desired, and serve hot.
Cauliflower	10 pounds	1 1/2 gallons	4 to 6 minutes	
Whole kernel corn	10 pounds	1 gallon	6 to 10 minutes	
Mustard or turnip greens	10 pounds	1 gallon	15 to 35 minutes	
Mixed vegetables	10 pounds	1 gallon	10 to 14 minutes	
Okra	10 pounds	1 gallon	5 to 8 minutes	
Peas or peas and carrots	10 pounds	3 quarts	8 to 10 minutes	
Spinach	10 pounds	1 quart	5 to 10 minutes	
Summer squash	10 pounds	1 quart	10 minutes	
Succotash	10 pounds	1 gallon	12 to 14 minutes	

Sauces, Gravies, and Dressings

Cream or White Sauce 164
    Cheese Sauce 165
    Egg Sauce 165
    Fricassee Sauce 165
    Supreme Sauce 165
    Horseradish Sauce 165
    Mustard Sauce 165
Horseradish Whipped Cream Sauce 166
Brown Gravy 167
    Chicken or Turkey Gravy 167
    Cream Gravy 167
    Giblet Gravy 167
    Onion Gravy 167
    Vegetable Gravy 167
    Tomato Gravy 167
Natural Pan Gravy 168
Bread Dressing 169
    Apple Sage Dressing................................. 169
    Giblet Dressing 169
    Chestnut Dressing 169
    Raisin Dressing 169
Cornbread Dressing (Southern) 170

CREAM OR WHITE SAUCE

YIELD: About 1 gallon
PAN SIZE: Heavy 6-quart saucepan or double boiler
PORTION SIZE:
TEMPERATURE:

INGREDIENTS	WEIGHTS/MEASURES	FOR____	METHOD
THIN Melted butter or margarine All-purpose flour	 1 cup 1 cup		1. Mix melted butter or margarine and flour together until smooth.
MEDIUM Melted butter or margarine All-purpose flour	 2 cups 2 cups		
THICK Melted butter or margarine All-purpose flour	 3 cups 1 quart		
Nonfat dry milk Hot water Salt	$1\frac{1}{4}$ quarts $3\frac{3}{4}$ quarts 2 tablespoons		2. Stir dry milk into water and heat to just below boiling. DO NOT BOIL. 3. Add flour mixture to hot milk, stirring constantly. Add salt and cook and stir over medium heat until smooth and thickened. Continue to cook over low heat, stirring constantly, about 8 to 10 minutes or until the starchy taste is gone. (The sauce can be put into a double boiler after it is thickened and cooked over simmering water, stirring occasionally, until the starchy taste is gone.)

NOTES: Several methods of preparing cream sauce are used in the recipes in this book in order to acquaint users with the different methods. This method is considered the simplest and easiest. The use of a whip instead of a spoon also helps in preparing the sauce. See the following page for variations of this basic sauce and for dietary information.

Variations:

1. *CHEESE SAUCE:* Add 1 pound grated or shredded cheddar, American process, or Swiss cheese, 1 tablespoon salad mustard, 1 teaspoon Worcestershire sauce, and ¼ teaspoon white pepper after step 3. Stir until cheese is melted and serve hot.
2. *EGG SAUCE:* Add 12 hard-cooked eggs and 1½ tablespoons salad mustard after step 3. Serve hot.
3. *FRICASSEE SAUCE:* Add 1 cup finely chopped onions in step 1. Use 1 gallon chicken or turkey stock which has been chilled and had the fat removed instead of the nonfat dry milk, water, and salt in step 2. Add ⅓ cup chopped pimiento and ¼ teaspoon of pepper after step 2. Taste for seasoning and add salt to taste. Serve hot.
4. *SUPREME SAUCE:* Use 2 quarts milk and 2 quarts coffee cream (18%) instead of nonfat dry milk and water in step 2. Beat 3 egg yolks slightly. Stir 1 cup hot sauce into the egg yolks. Mix well and stir back into the sauce. Serve hot.
5. *HORSERADISH SAUCE:* Beat 3 egg yolks slightly. Stir 1 cup hot sauce into the egg yolks. Mix well and stir back into the sauce. Stir ½ cup grated horseradish into the sauce and serve hot.
6. *MUSTARD SAUCE:* Add ½ cup salad mustard after step 3 and serve hot.

DIETARY INFORMATION:

May be used as written for general, bland, soft, and mild 2- to 3-gram sodium-restricted diets.
Diabetic: The recipe provides the following per ¼ cup serving:
    Thin white sauce: 30 calories or ½ bread exchange.
    Medium white sauce: 60 calories or 1 bread exchange.
    Thick white sauce: 80 calories or about 1½ bread exchanges.
Low-cholesterol: Use margarine in step 1.

HORSERADISH WHIPPED CREAM SAUCE

YIELD: About 3 quarts
PAN SIZE:
PORTION SIZE:
TEMPERATURE:

INGREDIENTS	WEIGHTS/MEASURES	FOR _____	METHOD
Heavy whipping cream	1 quart		1. Chill whipping cream, whip, and mixer bowl. 2. Beat cream at high speed until cream holds its shape.
Salt Drained prepared horseradish Prepared mustard Mayonnaise or salad dressing White pepper	4 teaspoons 1 cup 1 tablespoon 1½ cups ⅛ teaspoon		3. Mix salt, horseradish, mustard, mayonnaise or salad dressing, and pepper together until smooth. Stir lightly into whipped cream. Refrigerate until served.

DIETARY INFORMATION:

May be used as written for general diets.

BROWN GRAVY

YIELD: About 1 gallon
PAN SIZE: Heavy 6-quart saucepan
PORTION SIZE:
TEMPERATURE:

INGREDIENTS	WEIGHTS/MEASURES	FOR ___	METHOD
Fat from meat drippings or shortening All-purpose flour	2 cups 2 cups		1. Melt fat. Add flour and cook and stir over medium heat until browned and smooth. Remove from heat and cool.
Fat-free stock or drippings or a combination of them and water Salt Pepper (optional)	1 gallon As necessary $\frac{1}{8}$ teaspoon		2. Put stock, drippings, and water in saucepan. Add salt to taste and pepper. Heat to a simmer. Add flour mixture (roux), stirring constantly. Simmer 10 minutes or until thickened and the starchy taste is gone. Serve hot.

Variations:

1. *CHICKEN or TURKEY GRAVY:* Use chicken or turkey fat and stock instead of fat from meat drippings or shortening and other stock.
2. *CREAM GRAVY:* Do not brown the flour and fat in step 1. Add 1 quart of nonfat dry milk to stock in step 2. Mix well and then add the flour mixture. DO NOT BOIL THE MILK BEFORE THE FLOUR IS ADDED.
3. *GIBLET GRAVY:* Add 3 cups chopped, cooked giblets to chicken or turkey gravy in step 2.
4. *ONION GRAVY:* Brown 1 quart finely chopped onions in fat before adding flour in step 1.
5. *VEGETABLE GRAVY:* Add 1 quart drained canned mixed vegetables after step 2.
6. *TOMATO GRAVY:* Add $3\frac{1}{2}$ cups (one No. $2\frac{1}{2}$ can) tomato sauce to hot stock and use instead of the fat-free stock or drippings in step 2.

DIETARY INFORMATION:
May be used as written for general diets.
May be used as written for bland and soft diets if the pepper is not used in step 2.
Diabetic: This recipe provides 2 fat exchanges per $\frac{1}{4}$-cup portion.

NOTES:
This is a medium thick gravy. If a thinner gravy is desired, use $1\frac{1}{2}$ cups all-purpose flour in step 1.

NATURAL PAN GRAVY

YIELD: About 1 gallon
PAN SIZE: Heavy 6-quart saucepan

PORTION SIZE:
TEMPERATURE:

INGREDIENTS	WEIGHTS/MEASURES	FOR ____	METHOD
Hot drippings and meat juices Boiling water	3 quarts 1 quart		1. Skim any excess fat from meat drippings. Add water to drippings in the pan. Stir and scrape the bottoms and sides of roasting pan until drippings, water, and brown particles are well blended. Measure and pour into saucepan.
Worcestershire sauce Salt Pepper	¼ cup 1 tablespoon ½ teaspoon		2. Add Worcestershire sauce, salt, and pepper to drippings using the amounts given here for 1 gallon hot drippings and meat juices. Heat stock over medium heat and serve hot.

DIETARY INFORMATION:

May be used as written for general, low-fat, low-cholesterol, and soft diets.
Diabetic: This recipe does not provide any exchanges which must be counted for the diabetic diet.

BREAD DRESSING

YIELD: 50 portions (about 1½ gallons)　　　**PORTION SIZE:** ½ cup
PAN SIZE: Roaster　　　**TEMPERATURE:** 350°F Oven

INGREDIENTS	WEIGHTS/MEASURES	FOR_____	METHOD
Finely chopped celery Finely chopped onions Chicken fat, butter, or margarine	1½ quarts 3 cups 2 cups (1 pound)		1. Fry celery and onions in fat over medium heat, stirring frequently, until onions are golden.
Diced day-old white bread	3 gallons (5 pounds)		2. Pour vegetables and fat over diced bread. Toss lightly.
Fat-free salted chicken broth Slightly beaten eggs Salt Pepper Ground sage	3 quarts 1½ cups (7 to 8 medium) 2 teaspoons 1 teaspoon 1½ tablespoons		3. Combine broth, eggs, salt, pepper, and sage. Mix to blend and pour over bread mixture. Toss lightly but thoroughly. Do not overmix. 4. Place dressing in well-greased roaster. Bake 1½ hours or until top is browned. Serve hot.

DIETARY INFORMATION:

May be used as written for general diets.
Diabetic: This recipe provides 1 bread and 2 fat exchanges per portion.
Low-cholesterol: Use margarine in step 1, and 1 cup of egg whites instead of whole eggs in step 4.

NOTES:

Variations:
1. *APPLE SAGE DRESSING:* Add 1 quart of chopped canned or fresh apples in step 2.
2. *GIBLET DRESSING:* Add 3 cups cooked chopped giblets in step 2.
3. *CHESTNUT DRESSING:* Cook, peel, and chop 1 pound chestnuts and add in step 2.
4. *RAISIN DRESSING:* Add 2 cups washed and drained raisins in step 2.

CORNBREAD DRESSING
(Southern)

YIELD: 50 portions (1 pan)
PAN SIZE: 12 × 20 × 2-inch steam table pan
PORTION SIZE: ½ cup
TEMPERATURE: 350°F Oven

INGREDIENTS	WEIGHTS/MEASURES	FOR ___	METHOD
Finely chopped celery Finely chopped onions Chicken fat or vegetable oil	1 quart 1 quart 1 cup		1. Fry celery and onions in fat in heavy frying pan over medium heat, stirring frequently, until onions are golden.

Lukewarm fat-free
    chicken stock
Slightly beaten eggs
Salt
Melted margarine or
    chicken fat
Poultry seasoning
	2½ quarts
	1 cup (5 medium)
	1½ tablespoons
	
	1 cup
	2 tablespoons
			2. Combine stock, eggs, salt, melted fat, and poultry seasoning. Add fried celery and onions along with the fat in which they were fried. Mix lightly.

Diced day-old bread Coarse crumbs from day-old cornbread	1½ gallons (3 pounds) 3 quarts (2 pounds 4 ounces)		3. Place breads in large bowl. Pour chicken stock mixture evenly over breads. Mix lightly but thoroughly. 4. Spread dressing mixture evenly in well buttered steam table pan. 5. Bake about 1½ hours or until top is browned. Serve hot with giblet, turkey, or chicken gravy.

DIETARY INFORMATION:

May be used as written for general diets.

Cakes and Cookies

Apple Nut Squares	173
Applesauce Graham Cake	174
Chocolate Chip Date Cake (California)	175
Cinnamon Crunch Cake	176
Gingerbread	178
Molded Rainbow Cake	179
Raspberry Devil's Food Cake	180
Buttercream Frosting	181
Chocolate Buttercream Frosting	181
Orange Buttercream Frosting	181
Chocolate Fudge Frosting	182
Chocolate Nut Fudge Frosting	182
Chocolate Rum Frosting	182
Applesauce Cookies (Midwestern)	183
Chocolate Chip Peanut Butter Cookies	184
Chocolate Fudge Brownies	185
Margarine Cookies	186
Jewel Cookies	186
Frosted Cookies	186
Molasses Cookies (Midwestern)	187
Crisp Spice Cookies (New England)	188

Information

Although it is not always possible to bake cakes or cookies in the kitchen because of the shortage of time and help, it is a good idea to prepare them occasionally. Cake mixes are wonderful and have a place in every kitchen, and many things can be accomplished with cakes and cookies from bakeries. However, "from-scratch" cakes or cookies build a reputation for caring about the quality of food served.

Cakes and cookies are not difficult to prepare if a few basic rules are followed:

1. Recipes should be read thoroughly and understood before preparation is started. All ingredients and equipment should be available, and it is often a good idea to start preheating the oven before any actual mixing is started.
2. Regulation measuring cups and spoons should be used, and cakes should be baked in the specified-size pan.
3. Ingredients should be at room temperature unless directed otherwise by the recipe.
4. Ingredients should not be deleted or substitutions used unless the substitution ratios are understood.
5. Flour should not be sifted unless sifted flour is included in the wording of the recipe, since measurements for sifted and unsifted flours differ.
6. The oven door should not be opened until the end of the baking time specified in the recipe. If the cake is not done, it should be baked another 5 minutes and then tested again. Cakes may be tested with a cake tester, which will come out clean from the center of the cake. Most cakes can also be touched lightly in the center and will spring back if done.
7. Cookies should not be overbaked. Overbaked cookies will lose their flavor rapidly.
8. Generally, cookies should be loosened from the pan after they are baked and allowed to cool on racks, because they will continue to bake if left on the hot pans and will be difficult to remove from the pans.
9. Instructions should be followed regarding greasing cookie sheets. Cookies spread more evenly on greased pans. Some cookie recipes have enough fat in them that they don't need a greased pan, but others do need lightly greased pans.
10. Cookies should be baked on cool pans. Cookie pans may be lined with aluminum foil and the cookies placed on the aluminum foil to make cleanup easier, but the dough should not be put on aluminum foil and then put onto hot pans and baked.
11. Cookies on the same sheet pan should all be of uniform size so they will bake evenly. If there is not enough dough for a full pan of cookies, cookies should be baked in a smaller pan or put onto the center of the pan.

APPLE NUT SQUARES

YIELD: 54 portions (2 pans)
PAN SIZE: 12 × 18-inch cake pans

PORTION SIZE: 1 square
TEMPERATURE: 350°F Oven

INGREDIENTS	WEIGHTS/MEASURES	FOR _____	METHOD
All-purpose flour Baking soda Ground cinnamon Salt	2 quarts 4 teaspoons 4 teaspoons 2 teaspoons		1. Place flour, soda, cinnamon, and salt in mixer bowl. Mix at low speed for 1 minute to blend.
Crisp tart apples Lemon juice Chopped pecans	1 gallon (5 to 6 pounds) ¼ cup 1 quart		2. Wash, core, and dice apples (do not peel). Sprinkle with lemon juice. Mix apples and nuts. Keep for use in step 3.
Eggs Sugar Vegetable oil	2½ cups (12 to 13 medium) 1¾ quarts 1 quart		3. Beat eggs, sugar, and oil together to blend. Add to flour mixture. Beat at medium speed for 1 minute. Add apples and nuts to batter. Mix at low speed about one half minute. 4. Spread one half of the batter in each of 2 buttered and floured cake pans. 5. Bake 1 hour. Cool to room temperature.
Powdered sugar (optional)	¼ cup		6. Sprinkle powdered sugar evenly over cakes. Cut each 3 × 9.

DIETARY INFORMATION:
May be used as written for general, high-fiber, and mild 2- to 3-gram sodium-restricted diets.

NOTES: This recipe was furnished by South Chicago Hospital Dietary Department, Chicago, Illinois.

APPLESAUCE GRAHAM CAKE

YIELD: 54 portions (2 pans)
PAN SIZE: 12 × 18-inch cake pans

PORTION SIZE: 1 piece
TEMPERATURE: 375°F Oven

INGREDIENTS	WEIGHTS/MEASURES	FOR _____	METHOD
Sugar Shortening Eggs Vanilla	1¼ quarts 2 cups 1 cup (5 medium) 2 tablespoons		1. Cream sugar, shortening, eggs, and vanilla together until light.
All-purpose flour Graham flour Baking soda Ground cinnamon Ground cloves Salt	1½ quarts 1 quart 2 tablespoons 1 tablespoon 1 tablespoon 1 tablespoon		2. Stir flours, soda, cinnamon, cloves, and salt together to blend.
Applesauce	1½ quarts		3. Add applesauce and flour mixture together to creamed mixture. Beat 2 minutes at medium speed.
Chopped nuts Washed and drained raisins	1 quart 1 quart		4. Add nuts and raisins to batter. Mix at low speed only until nuts and raisins are distributed throughout the batter. 5. Spread one half of the batter evenly in each of 2 buttered and floured cake pans. 6. Bake 40 to 45 minutes or until cake tester comes out clean. 7. Cool cake and frost with butter cream frosting. Cut each cake 6 × 4.

DIETARY INFORMATION:

May be used for general, high-fiber, and mild 2- to 3-gram sodium-restricted diets.

CHOCOLATE CHIP DATE CAKE
(California)

YIELD: 54 portions (2 pans)
PAN SIZE: 12 × 18-inch cake pans
PORTION SIZE: 1 piece
TEMPERATURE: 350°F Oven

INGREDIENTS	WEIGHTS/MEASURES	FOR _____	METHOD
Chopped pitted dates Boiling water	3½ cups (1 pound) 1 quart		1. Mix dates and boiling water gently. Let stand 15 minutes. Do not cook dates and water.
Shortening Sugar Vanilla Eggs	2⅔ cups 1¼ quarts 2 tablespoons 2 cups (10 medium)		2. Cream shortening, sugar, vanilla, and eggs together until light and fluffy.
All-purpose flour Cocoa Baking soda	1¾ quarts ¼ cup 4 teaspoons		3. Stir flour, cocoa, and soda together to blend. Add to creamed mixture and beat 3 minutes at low speed.
Chopped nuts Chocolate chips Powdered sugar (optional)	2 cups 1 quart (2 12-ounce packages) ½ cup		4. Stir date mixture, chocolate chips, and nuts into batter. Spread one half of the batter evenly in each of 2 buttered cake pans. 5. Bake 40 minutes. Cool in pan on a wire rack. Springkle with powdered sugar. 6. Cut each pan 3 × 9.

DIETARY INFORMATION:

May be used as written for general, high-fiber, and mild 2- to 3-gram sodium-restricted diets.

CINNAMON CRUNCH CAKE

YIELD: 54 portions (2 pans)
PAN SIZE: 12 × 18-inch cake pans
PORTION SIZE: 1 piece
TEMPERATURE: 375°F Oven

INGREDIENTS	WEIGHTS/MEASURES	FOR ___	METHOD
Coarsely chopped nuts Softened butter or margarine Brown sugar All Bran or Bran Buds Ground cinnamon	3 cups 3 cups (1 pound 8 ounces) 3 cups 3 cups 1½ tablespoons		1. Combine nuts, butter or margarine, brown sugar, bran, and cinnamon in mixer bowl. Mix at low speed about 2 minutes or until well blended. Pat one half of the mixture evenly in the bottom of each of 2 cake pans which have been lined with well-buttered brown paper or aluminum foil. Set aside for use in step 6.
Shortening Brown sugar	3 cups 1½ quarts		2. Cream shortening and brown sugar together until light and fluffy.
Eggs	2 cups (10 medium)		3. Add eggs to creamed mixture. Mix at medium speed for 1 minute.
All-purpose flour Baking powder Salt Ground cinnamon	3 quarts ¼ cup 2 teaspoons 2 tablespoons		4. Stir flour, baking powder, salt, and cinnamon together to blend.
Milk	1½ quarts		5. Add flour mixture to batter alternately with milk, starting and finishing with milk. Mix 2 minutes at medium speed. Stop mixer twice during mixing to scrape down bowl.
All Bran or Bran Buds Whipped topping or vanilla ice cream	2 cups As desired		6. Stir bran into batter. Spread half of the batter evenly on top of the brown sugar mixture in each pan. 7. Bake 35 to 45 minutes or until cake tester comes out clean from the center of the cake.

(Continued)

INGREDIENTS	WEIGHTS/MEASURES	FOR_____	METHOD
			8. Let cake set for 10 minutes. Turn out and serve crunchy side up. Cut each pan 3 × 9 and serve with whipped topping or ice cream if desired.

DIETARY INFORMATION:

May be used as written for general and high-fiber diets.

GINGERBREAD

YIELD: 54 portions (2 pans)
PAN SIZE: 12 × 18-inch cake pans
PORTION SIZE: 1 piece
TEMPERATURE: 350°F Oven

INGREDIENTS	WEIGHTS/MEASURES	FOR _____	METHOD
Shortening Sugar	2½ cups 2 cups		1. Cream shortening and sugar together until light and fluffy.
Molasses Eggs	1 quart 1½ cups (7 to 8 medium)		2. Add molasses and eggs to creamed mixture. Beat at medium speed for 1 minute. Scrape down bowl and beat for another ½ minute.
All-purpose flour Ground cinnamon Ground ginger Salt Baking soda	10½ cups 1 tablespoon 1 tablespoon 1½ teaspoons 2½ teaspoons		3. Stir flour, cinnamon, ginger, salt, and soda together to blend.
Hot water Ice cream, whipped cream, whipped topping, or applesauce	1 quart As desired		4. Add all of the flour mixture and then all of the hot water to the creamed mixture. Beat 2 minutes at medium speed or until smooth. 5. Spread one half of the batter into each of 2 buttered and floured cake pans. 6. Bake 40 to 45 minutes or until a cake tester comes out clean. Cut each pan 9 × 3. 7. Serve warm, topped with ice cream, whipped cream, whipped topping, or applesauce.

DIETARY INFORMATION:

May be used as written for general, bland, soft, and mild 2- to 3-gram sodium-restricted diets.

MOLDED RAINBOW CAKE

YIELD: 1 pan
PAN SIZE: 12 × 20 × 2-inch steam table pan
PORTION SIZE:
TEMPERATURE: 350°F Oven

INGREDIENTS	WEIGHTS/MEASURES	FOR ____	METHOD
3-ounce packages assorted flavored gelatin	4		1. Prepare gelatin as directed on package, putting each flavor gelatin in a separate pan. Different size pans may be used but a 9-inch square pan for each flavor will yield the most uniform cubes. Chill gelatin until firm. Cut into cubes and reserve for use in step 4. An assortment of colors and flavors will add a rainbow look to the cake.
Graham cracker crumbs Sugar Softened margarine	2¼ cups (8 ounces) ¼ cup ½ cup (1 stick)		2. Combine crumbs, sugar, and margarine. Mix well. Press evenly into the bottom of steam table pan. Bake 5 minutes. Cool to room temperature.
Lemon-flavored gelatin Sugar Boiling hot pineapple juice	1 cup (7 ounces) ½ cup 2 cups		3. Dissolve gelatin and sugar in pineapple juice. Chill until slightly thickened.
Prepared whipped topping	2 quarts		4. Fold slightly thickened gelatin into whipped topping. Add gelatin cubes. Chill if necessary until mixture will mound. Pour into graham cracker crust. Chill about 3 hours or until firm. 5. Cut into squares and serve cold.

DIETARY INFORMATION:

May be used as written for general, bland, soft, and mild 2- to 3-gram sodium-restricted diets.

RASPBERRY DEVIL'S FOOD CAKE

YIELD: 48 portions (one 2-layer cake)
PAN SIZE: 12 × 18-inch cake pans

PORTION SIZE: 1 piece
TEMPERATURE: 350°F Oven

INGREDIENTS	WEIGHTS/MEASURES	FOR ____	METHOD
Baking chocolate	1 pound (16 squares)		1. Melt chocolate in the top of a double boiler over simmering water.
All-purpose flour Sugar Salt Baking soda Baking powder	2 quarts 2 quarts 2 teaspoons 4 teaspoons 2 teaspoons		2. Place flour, sugar, salt, soda, and baking powder in mixer bowl. Mix at low speed for 1 minute to blend.
Sour cream Eggs Vanilla Water Softened shortening	1 quart 1½ cups (7 to 8 medium) 2 tablespoons 2⅔ cups 2 cups		3. Add melted chocolate, sour cream, eggs, vanilla, water, and shortening to flour mixture in the order listed. Beat at medium speed for 3 to 4 minutes or until smooth and well blended. Scrape down bowl once during mixing. 4. Spread one half of the batter evenly in each of 2 buttered and floured cake pans. 5. Bake about 40 minutes or until a cake tester comes out clean from the center. Let stand 10 minutes in the pans and then turn out on rack to finish cooling.
Raspberry jam	3 cups		6. Turn one of the cakes upside down on a surface which has been dusted with sugar. Spread jam evenly over the top of the layer. 7. Place remaining layer, top side up, on top of the jam. Frost cake with chocolate fudge frosting. (See page 182.) 8. Cut cake 4 × 12 and serve.

DIETARY INFORMATION:
May be used as written for general and bland diets.

NOTES: Cherry, strawberry, or apricot jam may be used instead of raspberry jam in step 6.

BUTTERCREAM FROSTING

YIELD: 1¼ quarts (frosts 1 sheet cake, 6 dozen cupcakes, or three 2-layer cakes)

PORTION SIZE:

TEMPERATURE:

INGREDIENTS	WEIGHTS/MEASURES	FOR ___	METHOD
Butter or margarine	1 cup (2 sticks)		1. Cream butter or margarine in mixer bowl until soft and creamy, using beater at medium speed.
Powdered sugar Salt Nonfat dry milk Vanilla Water	1¾ quarts (2 pounds) ½ teaspoon ¼ cup 1 tablespoon ¼ to ⅓ cup		2. Stir sugar, salt, and dry milk together. Add with vanilla to butter or margarine. Add water while beating at low speed. Scrape down bowl. Beat another minute at low speed or until frosting has the desired consistency. 3. Spread frosting on cool cake.

DIETARY INFORMATION:

May be used as written for general, bland, soft, and mild 2- to 3-gram sodium-restricted diets.

Low-cholesterol: Use margarine instead of butter in step 1. Variations may also be used if margarine is used.

NOTES:

Variations:
1. *CHOCOLATE:* Add ¼ cup cocoa in step 2 and use about ½ cup boiling water in step 2.
2. *ORANGE:* Omit dry milk, water, and vanilla in step 2. Add 2 tablespoons grated orange rind and ⅓ cup orange juice in step 2.

CHOCOLATE FUDGE FROSTING

YIELD: 1¼ quarts (frosts 1 sheet cake, 6 dozen cupcakes, or three 2-layer cakes)

PORTION SIZE:

TEMPERATURE:

INGREDIENTS	WEIGHTS/MEASURES	FOR ___	METHOD
Softened butter or margarine	1 cup (2 sticks)		1. Place butter or margarine, sugar, salt, cocoa, and vanilla in mixer bowl.
Powdered sugar	1¾ quarts (2 pounds)		
Salt	½ teaspoon		
Cocoa	1 cup		
Vanilla	1 tablespoon		
Light corn syrup	½ cup		2. Combine syrup and water. Heat to simmering but do not boil. Add to powdered sugar mixture in mixer bowl. Beat at low speed until smooth.
Hot water	¼ cup		3. Spread warm frosting on cool cake. The frosting will spread if it is cool but it won't be as glossy as it will be if you spread it while it is still warm.

DIETARY INFORMATION:

May be used as written for general, bland, soft, and mild 2- to 3-gram sodium-restricted diets.

Low-cholesterol: Use margarine instead of butter in step 1. Variations may be used if margarine is used.

NOTES:

Variations:
1. *CHOCOLATE NUT:* Add 2 cups chopped nuts to frosting after step 2.
2. *CHOCOLATE RUM:* Add 1 tablespoon of rum flavoring to frosting with vanilla in step 1.

APPLESAUCE COOKIES
(Midwestern)

YIELD: About 6 dozen cookies
PAN SIZE: 18 × 26-inch sheet pans
PORTION SIZE:
TEMPERATURE: 375°F Oven

INGREDIENTS	WEIGHTS/MEASURES	FOR ____	METHOD
Margarine Brown sugar Sugar	1 cup (2 sticks) 1 cup 1 cup		1. Cream margarine and sugars together at medium speed about 3 minutes or until light and fluffy.
Applesauce	2 cups		2. Add applesauce to creamed mixture and beat 1 minute at medium speed.
Sifted all-purpose flour Ground cinnamon Ground nutmeg Baking powder Baking soda	1 quart 2 teaspoons 1 teaspoon 2 teaspoons 2 teaspoons		3. Stir flour, cinnamon, nutmeg, baking powder, and soda together and add to dough. Beat 2 minutes at medium speed scraping down the bowl once during the mixing period.
Rolled oats Washed and drained raisins	1 quart 3 cups		4. Add rolled oats and raisins to dough and mix only until blended. Use a No. 40 dipper to drop the dough onto a sheet pan which has been lightly greased with margarine. Press the top of each cookie with the bottom of a glass which has been dipped in water and then in sugar until the dough is about ¼-inch thick. 5. Bake cookies 18 to 20 minutes or until lightly browned. Remove from pan onto wire rack while cookies are still warm.

DIETARY INFORMATION:

May be used as written for general, high-fiber, bland, and mild 2- to 3-gram sodium-restricted diets.

CHOCOLATE CHIP PEANUT BUTTER COOKIES

YIELD: 5 dozen cookies　　　　　　　　　　　　　　**PORTION SIZE:**

PAN SIZE: 18 × 26-inch sheet pans　　　　　　　　**TEMPERATURE:** 375°F Oven

INGREDIENTS	WEIGHTS/MEASURES	FOR___	METHOD
Margarine Sugar Smooth peanut butter	1 cup (2 sticks) 2 cups 1 cup		1. Cream margarine, sugar, and peanut butter together until light and fluffy.
Eggs Milk	½ cup (2 to 3 medium) ¼ cup		2. Add eggs and milk to creamed mixture. Beat at low speed for ½ minute to blend.
All-purpose flour Salt Baking soda	2¼ cups 1 teaspoon 1 teaspoon		3. Stir flour, salt, and soda together. Add to creamed mixture and beat 1 minute at low speed to blend.
Chocolate chips	2 cups (12-ounce package)		4. Add chocolate chips to dough. Beat at low speed only until chips are distributed throughout dough. 5. Drop dough by heaping tablespoonfuls (No. 40 dipper) onto lightly buttered sheet pan. 6. Bake 10 to 12 minutes or until lightly browned. Remove cookies from pan onto wire rack while cookies are still warm.

DIETARY INFORMATION:

May be used as written for general, high-fiber, bland, soft, and mild 2- to 3-gram sodium-restricted diets.

CHOCOLATE FUDGE BROWNIES

YIELD: 1 pan
PAN SIZE: 18 × 26-inch sheet pan
PORTION SIZE:
TEMPERATURE: 375°F Oven

INGREDIENTS	WEIGHTS/MEASURES	FOR _____	METHOD
Shortening Baking chocolate Sugar	3 cups 12 ounces (12 squares) 1½ quarts		1. Melt shortening and chocolate in top of double boiler over simmering water. Add sugar and mix well. Place mixture in mixer bowl and cool to lukewarm.
Eggs	2½ cups (12 to 13 medium)		2. Add eggs to chocolate mixture 2 at a time, beating 1 minute at medium speed after each addition.
Sifted all-purpose flour Salt	4½ cups 1 tablespoon		3. Add flour and salt to batter. Mix 1 minute at medium speed. Scrape down bowl and beat another minute.
Chopped nuts Vanilla	1 quart (1 pound) 2 tablespoons		4. Add nuts and vanilla to batter. Spread batter evenly in lightly greased sheet pan. 5. Bake 30 minutes or until slightly firm to the touch. Do not overbake. 6. Brownies should be cut while they are still slightly warm. They can be frosted with Chocolate Fudge or Buttercream Frosting (see pages 181 and 182).

DIETARY INFORMATION:

May be used as written for general diets.

MARGARINE COOKIES

YIELD: 5 dozen cookies
PAN SIZE: 18 × 26-inch sheet pans
PORTION SIZE:
TEMPERATURE: 375°F Oven

INGREDIENTS	WEIGHTS/MEASURES	FOR ___	METHOD
Margarine Powdered sugar	1 cup (2 sticks) 1¼ cups		1. Cream margarine and powdered sugar together until light and fluffy.
Egg whites Vanilla	¼ cup (2 to 3 medium) 2 teaspoons		2. Add egg whites and vanilla gradually to creamed mixture. Beat 1 minute at medium speed.
Cake flour Baking soda Cream of tartar Salt	3 cups 1 teaspoon 1½ teaspoons ¼ teaspoon		3. Sift flour, soda, cream of tartar, and salt together. Add to creamed mixture and mix at low speed about 1 minute until smooth. 4. Put dough in pastry bag and bag cookies on sheet pan in desired shapes. Let stand in cool place or refrigerate 2 hours before baking. 5. Bake 8 to 10 minutes or until lightly browned. Remove to wire racks while slightly warm.

DIETARY INFORMATION:

May be used as written for general, low-cholesterol, bland, soft, or mild 2- to 3-gram sodium-restricted diets.

NOTES:

Variations:
1. *JEWEL COOKIES:* Add 1½ cups chopped candied cherries or mixed candied fruit to dough. Drop by teaspoonful onto sheet pans. Bake 8 to 10 minutes.
2. *FROSTED COOKIES:* Frost cookies after they are cool, using one of the frostings in this book or other favorite frosting.

MOLASSES COOKIES
(Midwestern)

YIELD: About 10 dozen cookies
PAN SIZE: 18 × 26-inch sheet pans
PORTION SIZE:
TEMPERATURE: 400°F Oven

INGREDIENTS	WEIGHTS/MEASURES	FOR ___	METHOD
Margarine Sugar Molasses	2 cups (1 pound) 2 cups 2 cups		1. Cream margarine and sugar together until light and fluffy. Add molasses and mix 1 minute at medium speed to blend.
All-purpose flour Baking soda Ground ginger Ground cinnamon Boiling water	2¾ quarts 2 tablespoons 2 teaspoons 2 teaspoons 2 cups		2. Stir flour, soda, ginger, and cinnamon together. Add to creamed mixture alternately with boiling water. Mix at low speed for about 4 minutes to form a soft dough. 3. Drop dough by heaping tablespoonfuls (No. 40 dipper) onto sheet pans which have been lightly greased with margarine. Press the top of each cookie down with the bottom of a glass which has been dipped in water and then in sugar until the dough is about ¼ inch thick. 4. Bake about 15 minutes. Remove cookies from pan onto wire rack while still warm.

DIETARY INFORMATION:

May be used as written for general, soft, bland, low-cholesterol, and mild 2- to 3-gram sodium-restricted diets.

CRISP SPICE COOKIES
(New England)

YIELD: About 10 dozen cookies
PAN SIZE: 18 × 26-inch sheet pans
PORTION SIZE:
TEMPERATURE: 400°F Oven

INGREDIENTS	WEIGHTS/MEASURES	FOR ___	METHOD
Margarine Sugar Dark corn syrup	1 cup (2 sticks) 2 cups 1 cup		1. Cream margarine and sugar together until light and fluffy. Add syrup and continue to beat another minute.
All-purpose flour Baking soda Pumpkin pie spice Salt Boiling hot water	4½ cups 2 teaspoons 2 teaspoons ½ teaspoon ¾ cup		2. Stir flour, soda, spice, and salt together and add to creamed mixture. Add water and mix 1 minute at medium speed. Drop by heaping teaspoonfuls onto a pan which has been lightly greased with margarine. 3. Bake 8 to 10 minutes. Remove from pan onto a wire rack while cookies are still warm.

DIETARY INFORMATION:
May be used as written for general, low-cholesterol, soft, bland, and mild 2- to 3-gram sodium-restricted diets.

Pies and Puddings

Pie Crust	191
Margarine Pie Crust	193
Graham Pie Crust	194
Graham Cracker Crust	196
Meringue	197
Chess Pie (Texas)	198
Chocolate Pecan Pie	199
Chocolate Walnut Pie	199
Cranberry Cheese Pie (New England)	200
Jefferson Davis Pie (Southern)	201
Pecan Pie (Southern)	202
Mock Pecan Pie (Midwestern)	203
Shoofly Pie (Pennsylvania Dutch)	204
Sweet Potato Pie (Southern)	205
Baked Indian Pudding (New England)	207
Ozark Pudding (Missouri)	208
Raisin Nut Pudding Cake (Midwestern)	209

Information

Pies as we understand them are native to this country. The English have been using meat pies for centuries, but the use of fruit and cream fillings developed in this country. Therefore, the pies in this section are all native American recipes. Recipes for fruit pies and cream pies are not included, since those recipes are readily available along with commercial fillings which are economical and convenient to use.

In many cases it is the pie pastry or crust which makes a good pie and there are certain basic rules for making good pastry which should be followed with any recipe.

1. Most pie crust is made from flour, salt, fat, and water. Flakiness and tenderness are the most important characteristics of a good crust and both of these depend on the proportion of ingredients used and the method of mixing. Therefore, it is very important to follow the recipe exactly.
2. The flakiness of a pie crust depends on the method of mixing the shortening into the flour. A mealy texture will result if the shortening is mixed with the flour until the shortening is in very small particles. If the shortening is mixed with the flour until it is the size of giant peas, the crust will have a short flaky texture. If the shortening is left in marble-sized pieces the crust will be of the long flaky type.
3. Tenderness of a pie crust depends to a large extent on the proper handling of the pie dough. Since not all flours absorb the same quantity of liquid, the proper amount of liquid to use will vary. Use only a sufficient amount of water to make a soft pliable dough because excess water will cause the crust to become tough. Graham or whole-wheat dough will seem soft at first if sufficient water is used but will become more firm after standing because the bran continues to absorb water after it is mixed. Shortening should be soft enough to blend easily into the flour but not liquified. The water should be very cold when added, about 40°F or less.
4. Pie crusts may be mixed by hand or in the mixer. It is important to avoid overmixing in either method. Overmixing will toughen the crust and cause it to shrink while it is baking.
5. For a more tender product, crusts should be chilled after they are mixed.
6. Pie crust should not be allowed to stand in a warm room after it is mixed. It should be refrigerated until almost time to use it, allowed to come back to room temperature, and then used. Crusts which have been shaped and filled should be refrigerated if not baked immediately.
7. Pie dough should be rolled on a lightly floured board. Extra flour rolled into the crust will toughen it.
8. Dough should be eased gently into the pan, never stretched to fit the pan. The dough will shrink during baking if it is stretched.
9. A cooked filling should always be cooled before it is put into an unbaked crust. A hot filling will melt the fat in the crust and the crust will be tough.
10. The edge of the bottom crust of a two-crust pie is moistened before the top is laid on the filling to help seal the two crusts together and help prevent the filling from leaking out during baking.
11. Meringue should touch all of the inside edges of the crust to prevent it pulling away from the sides of the crust while it is baking.
12. Baking temperature for pies is very important. If the temperature is too low the crust will be tough, and if the temperature is too high the crust will brown too quickly and there will be a layer of uncooked dough on the inside of the crust.
13. Dough trimmings should be rolled into a ball and used for a bottom crust, never a top crust.

PIE CRUST

YIELD: Crust for eight 9-inch double crust pies or crust for twelve 9- or 10-inch pie shells

PAN SIZE: 9 or 10 × 1-inch pie pans

PORTION SIZE:

TEMPERATURE: 450°F Oven

INGREDIENTS	WEIGHTS/MEASURES	FOR_____	METHOD
All-purpose flour Cake flour Salt	2 quarts (2 pounds 4 ounces) 1¾ quarts (1 pound 14 ounces) 2 tablespoons		1. Place flours and salt together in mixer bowl. Mix at low speed for ½ minute to blend.
Shortening or lard	1¼ quarts (2 pounds 4 ounces)		2. Add shortening or lard to flour mixture. Mix at low speed for ½ to 1 minute or until fat resembles very large peas.
Very cold water (40°F)	3 to 3½ cups		3. Add 3 cups water to flour mixture. Mix at low speed as little as possible to form a stiff dough. Add part or all of the remaining ½ cup water if necessary. 4. Place dough on lightly floured working surface. Divide into eight portions of 9 ounces each and eight portions of 7 ounces each for double crust pies or twelve portions about 10 ounces each for single crust pies. Put dough on lightly floured pan and cover with plastic. Refrigerate from 1 hour to overnight. Remove from refrigerator and let dough return to room temperature. 5. Lightly dust each piece of dough with flour and flatten gently on a lightly floured working surface with the palm of the hand. With a floured rolling pin, roll lightly from the center out to the edge in all directions forming a circle about 1 inch wider than the pie tin for the top and about 2 inches wider than the pan for the bottom.

(Continued)

INGREDIENTS	WEIGHTS/MEASURES	FOR ____	METHOD
			6. Fold pastry circle in half and lift it into the pie pan with the fold in the center. Unfold and press the pastry to the bottom and sides of the pan so it fits tightly but is not stretched. Lift pastry to let out air bubbles, if necessary. 7. Roll out top crust in the same way as bottom crust. Fold in half. Make several slits near the center fold with a knife to allow steam to escape during baking. 8. Fill bottom crust as directed by specific pie recipe. Brush outer rim of bottom crust with water. Lay top crust over filling with fold at center. Unfold and press edges of crusts together lightly. 9. Remove excess dough and seal edges together by pressing the palms of both hands against the rim of the pie, or finish as desired. Reserve any excess dough for other bottom crusts. Always use fresh dough for top crusts of pies. 10. Bake according to directions given with pie recipe or until lightly browned. 11. When making pie shells, prick the crust all over the bottom of the crust with the tines of a fork before baking about 10 minutes or until lightly browned.

DIETARY INFORMATION:

May be used as written for general, bland, soft, and mild 2- to 3-gram sodium-restricted diets.

MARGARINE PIE CRUST

YIELD: Crust for eight 9-inch double crust pies or crust for fourteen 9- or 10-inch pie shells

PAN SIZE: 9 or 10 × 1-inch pie pans

PORTION SIZE:

TEMPERATURE:

INGREDIENTS	WEIGHTS/MEASURES	FOR _____	METHOD
All-purpose flour Salt	3½ quarts (4 pounds) 1 tablespoon		1. Place flour and salt in mixer bowl. Mix at low speed for a few seconds to blend.
Firm margarine	6¼ cups (3 pounds 4 ounces)		2. Margarine should be allowed to come to room temperature before it is used and then cut into about 8 pieces to a 4-ounce stick before it is added to the flour. 3. Mix at low speed about ½ to 1 minute or until margarine is the size of large peas.
Very cold water (40°F)	2 to 4 cups		4. Add 2 cups water to flour and margarine mixture. (Various brands of margarine have a greater liquid content and therefore the amount of water necessary will vary greatly.) Mix at low speed as little as possible to form a stiff dough. Add as much of the remaining 2 cups of water as necessary. 5. Place dough on lightly floured surface. Divide into eight portions of 10 ounces each and eight portions of 8 ounces each for double crust pies or fourteen portions of about 10 ounces each for single crust pies. Place dough on lightly floured pan and cover with plastic. Refrigerate from 1 hour to overnight. Remove from refrigerator and let dough return to room temperature. 6. Follow steps 5 through 11 in recipe for Pie Crust on pages 191 and 192.

DIETARY INFORMATION:

May be used as written for general, low-cholesterol, soft, bland, and mild 2- to 3-gram sodium-restricted diets.

GRAHAM PIE CRUST

YIELD: Crusts for eight 9-inch double crust pies or crusts for fourteen 9- or 10-inch pie shells

PAN SIZE:

PORTION SIZE:

TEMPERATURE: 450°F Oven

INGREDIENTS	WEIGHTS/MEASURES	FOR _____	METHOD
All-purpose flour Graham flour Salt	2 quarts (2 pounds 4 ounces) 2 quarts (2 pounds 4 ounces) 2 tablespoons		1. Put flours and salt in mixer bowl. Mix at low speed for ½ minute to blend.
Shortening	1½ quarts (2 pounds 10 ounces)		2. Add shortening to flour mixture. Mix at low speed for ½ to 1 minute or until shortening resembles very large peas.
Very cold water (40°F)	3½ to 4 cups		3. Add 3½ cups water to flour mixture. Mix at low speed as little as possible to form a dough. Add all or part of the remaining ½ cup water, if necessary. Graham pie crust should not be quite as stiff as regular pie crust since the bran in the graham flour will absorb water as it stands for a period of time. 4. Place dough on a lightly floured surface. Divide into eight portions of 10 ounces each and eight portions of 8 ounces each for double crust pies or fourteen portions of about 10 ounces each for single crust pies. Place dough on lightly floured pan and cover with plastic. Refrigerate from 1 hour to overnight. Remove from refrigerator and let dough return to room temperature. 5. Follow steps 5 through 11 in recipe for Pie Crust on pages 191 and 192.

(continued)

DIETARY INFORMATION:

May be used as written for general, bland, soft, high-fiber, and mild 2- to 3-gram sodium-restricted diets.

NOTES:

1. This crust is particularly good with nut pies such as Pecan Pie or with cream fillings.
2. This crust recipe specifies graham flour. If whole wheat flour is used the weight will remain the same for the whole wheat flour as for the graham flour but the volume will be $1\frac{3}{4}$ quarts of whole wheat flour instead of 2 quarts graham flour.

GRAHAM CRACKER CRUST

YIELD: Eight 9-inch crusts
PAN SIZE: 9 × 1-inch pie pans

PORTION SIZE:
TEMPERATURE: 350°F

INGREDIENTS	WEIGHTS/MEASURES	FOR ___	METHOD
Butter or margarine	3 cups (1 pound 8 ounces)		1. Cream butter or margarine until light.
Graham cracker crumbs Sugar	2 pounds (2 quarts) 1¾ cups		2. Add crumbs and sugar to butter. Mix at medium speed until well blended. Do not overmix. 3. Use 1¾ cups (about 8 ounces) crumb mixture for each pie tin. Do not pack. Press firmly into an even layer against bottom and sides of pans. 4. Chill at least 1 hour before adding filling or if a firmer crust is desired, bake 7 to 8 minutes.

DIETARY INFORMATION:

May be used as written for general, bland, soft, and mild 2- to 3-gram sodium-restricted diets.

MERINGUE

YIELD: Meringue topping for eight 9-inch pies　　**PORTION SIZE:**
PAN SIZE:　　**TEMPERATURE:** 325°F Oven

INGREDIENTS	WEIGHTS/MEASURES	FOR___	METHOD
Egg whites	3 cups (about 24 to 27 medium)		1. Allow egg whites to come to room temperature in mixer bowl. 2. Beat egg whites 3 minutes at high speed using a whip, or until they hold a soft peak. It is important that egg whites, mixer, and bowl be free of egg yolk or fat of any kind.
Sugar Salt Vanilla	1 quart 1 teaspoon 2 teaspoons		3. Add sugar gradually to egg whites while beating at medium speed. Beat about 6 minutes at high speed or until meringue is stiff, glossy, and forms stiff peaks. Add salt and vanilla near the end of the beating period. 4. Spread one-eighth (about 2½ cups) of the meringue on each pie so that the meringue is sealed to the outside of the rim of the crust and the pie filling is completely covered. 5. Bake 15 to 20 minutes or until lightly browned.

DIETARY INFORMATION:

May be used as written for general, bland, soft, low-fat, low-cholesterol, and mild 2- to 3-gram sodium-restricted diets.

CHESS PIE
(Texas)

YIELD: 48 portions (six 9-inch pies)
PAN SIZE: 9-inch pie pans
PORTION SIZE: 1/8 pie
TEMPERATURE: 350°F Oven

INGREDIENTS	WEIGHTS/MEASURES	FOR ____	METHOD
Sugar All-purpose flour Cornmeal Salt Melted butter or margarine	2¼ quarts 1½ cups ¼ cup ½ teaspoon 2 cups (1 pound)		1. Place sugar, flour, cornmeal, and salt in mixer bowl. Mix at low speed for ½ minute to blend. Add melted butter or margarine and mix another ½ minute or until blended.
Eggs Buttermilk Vanilla Ground nutmeg	2½ cups (12 to 13 medium) 3 cups 1 tablespoon 1 teaspoon		2. Add eggs to sugar mixture and mix at medium speed until smooth and thickened. Add buttermilk, vanilla, and nutmeg. Mix at low speed only until blended.
Unbaked 9-inch pie shells	6		3. Pour one-sixth (about 2¾ to 3 cups) of the filling into each pie shell. 4. Bake 30 minutes or until center is firm. 5. Serve pie at room temperature, cutting each pie into 8 wedges.

DIETARY INFORMATION:

May be used as written for general, high-fiber, soft, bland, and mild 2- to 3-gram sodium-restricted diets.

NOTES: This recipe was furnished by Frances Lee, a consulting dietitian from Kerens, Texas, who says that many recipes for this pie use sweet milk but this version is the most popular in Texas.

CHOCOLATE PECAN PIE

YIELD: 48 portions (six 9-inch pies)
PAN SIZE: 9-inch pie pans
PORTION SIZE: 1/8 pie
TEMPERATURE: 375°F Oven

INGREDIENTS	WEIGHTS/MEASURES	FOR _____	METHOD
Margarine Sugar Eggs	1 cup (2 sticks) 1 quart 1¼ quarts (12 to 13 medium)		1. Cream margarine and sugar together until fluffy. Add eggs and beat at low speed for 1 minute or until well blended.
Cocoa Salt Vanilla Light corn syrup	1 cup 1½ teaspoons 2 tablespoons 2 quarts		2. Add cocoa, salt, vanilla, and syrup to creamed mixture. Beat at low speed for 3 minutes or until well blended.
Coarsely chopped pecans Unbaked 9-inch pie shells	2¼ quarts (2 pounds 4 ounces) 6		3. Put 1½ cups (6 ounces) coarsely chopped pecans in each pie shell. Add one-sixth (about 2½ cups) of the filling to each pie shell. 4. Bake 45 minutes to 1 hour or until crust is well browned. The crust should be built up around the edges because the filling puffs as it bakes. The center of the pie may be a little soft but it will become firmer as the pie cools. 5. Serve pie at room temperature, cutting each pie into 8 wedges.

DIETARY INFORMATION:

May be used as written for general, high-fiber, and mild 2- to 3-gram sodium-restricted diets.

NOTES:

Variation:
CHOCOLATE WALNUT PIE: Substitute walnuts for the pecans in step 3.

CRANBERRY CHEESE PIE
(New England)

YIELD: 48 portions (eight 9-inch pies) **PORTION SIZE:** 1/6 pie
PAN SIZE: 9-inch pie pans **TEMPERATURE:**

INGREDIENTS	WEIGHTS/MEASURES	FOR _____	METHOD
Fresh cranberries Water Frozen orange juice concentrate Salt	5 pounds 2½ quarts ½ cup 1 teaspoon		1. Wash cranberries well and look them over, discarding stems and any bruised or rotten cranberries. Place in heavy saucepan with water, orange juice concentrate, and salt. Simmer about 10 minutes, stirring occasionally.
Sugar Cornstarch	2½ quarts 1¼ cups		2. Mix sugar and cornstarch together. Pour slowly into cranberries while stirring constantly over medium heat. Continue to cook and stir about 10 minutes or until smooth and thickened and the starchy taste is gone. Cool to room temperature.
Cream cheese Lemon juice Prebaked 9-inch pie shells	4 pounds 1½ cups 8		3. Beat cream cheese and lemon juice together at low speed until blended. Spread one-eighth (about 1 cup) of the cheese mixture evenly in the bottom of each prebaked pie shell.
Whipped topping	1 gallon		4. Spoon one-eighth (about 2½ cups) of the cranberry mixture evenly over the cream cheese in each pie shell. Refrigerate at least ½ hour before serving. 5. Garnish each piece of pie with whipped topping, or spread 2 cups topping evenly over the top of each pie before serving.

DIETARY INFORMATION:

May be used as written for general, bland, and mild 2- to 3-gram sodium-restricted diets.

JEFFERSON DAVIS PIE
(Southern)

YIELD: 48 portions (six 9-inch pies)
PAN SIZE: 9-inch pie pans
PORTION SIZE: 1/8 pie
TEMPERATURE: 425° and 350°F Oven

INGREDIENTS	WEIGHTS/MEASURES	FOR _____	METHOD
Margarine Brown sugar	3 cups (1 pound 8 ounces) 3 quarts		1. Cream margarine and sugar together until light and fluffy.
Eggs	3 cups (15 medium)		2. Add eggs to creamed mixture. Beat at medium speed for 2 minutes
All-purpose flour Salt Vanilla Ground nutmeg	3/4 cup 1 1/2 teaspoons 2 tablespoons 1 tablespoon		3. Add flour, salt, vanilla, and nutmeg to creamed mixture. Beat 1 minute at low speed or until well blended.
Evaporated milk Chopped dates Coarsely chopped pecans Washed and drained raisins	1 1/2 quarts 1 1/2 cups 1 1/2 cups 1 1/2 cups		4. Add milk, dates, pecans, and raisins to filling. Mix at low speed for 1 minute.
Unbaked 9-inch pie shells	6		5. Pour one-sixth (about 1 quart) of the filling into each of the pie shells. 6. Bake at 425°F for 10 minutes. Decrease heat to 350°F and bake another 30 minutes. 7. Serve pie at room temperature, cutting each pie into 8 wedges.

DIETARY INFORMATION:

May be used as written for general, high-fiber, and mild 2- to 3-gram sodium-restricted diets.

NOTES: This pie is served with a meringue in some parts of the South.

PECAN PIE
(Southern)

YIELD: 48 portions (six 9-inch pies)
PAN SIZE: 9-inch pie pans
PORTION SIZE: 1/8 pie
TEMPERATURE: 350°F Oven

INGREDIENTS	WEIGHTS/MEASURES	FOR _____	METHOD
Eggs Sugar Melted butter or margarine	1¼ quarts (about 25 medium) 1¼ quarts ¾ cup (1½ sticks)		1. Place eggs in mixer bowl. Add sugar gradually while beating at medium speed. Beat until well blended. Add butter or margarine and beat another 1 to 2 minutes at medium speed.
Dark corn syrup Vanilla Salt	2 quarts 2 tablespoons 2 teaspoons		2. Add syrup, vanilla, and salt to filling. Mix at low speed only until smooth.
Coarsely chopped pecans Unbaked 9-inch pie shells	1½ quarts (about 1 pound 8 ounces) 6		3. Place 1 cup chopped pecans in each pie shell. Add one-sixth (about 2¾ cups) of the filling to each pie shell. The crust should be built up around the edges because the filling puffs as it bakes. 4. Bake 35 to 40 minutes or until filling is set. 5. Serve pie at room temperature, cutting each pie into 8 wedges.

DIETARY INFORMATION:

May be used as written for general, high-fiber, and mild 2- to 3-gram sodium-restricted diets.

MOCK PECAN PIE
(Midwestern)

YIELD: 48 portions (six 9-inch pies)
PAN SIZE: 9-inch pie pans
PORTION SIZE: 1/8 pie
TEMPERATURE: 350°F Oven

INGREDIENTS	WEIGHTS/MEASURES	FOR ___	METHOD
Butter or margarine Sugar	1½ cups (3 sticks) 3 cups		1. Cream butter or margarine and sugar together until light and fluffy.
Dark corn syrup Ground cinnamon Salt	1½ quarts 2 teaspoons 1½ teaspoons		2. Add syrup, cinnamon, and salt to creamed mixture. Mix at low speed 1 minute or until blended.
Eggs	3 cups (15 medium)		3. Add eggs to creamed mixture. Beat at medium speed for 3 minutes.
Rolled oats	1½ quarts		4. Add oatmeal to filling. Beat ½ minute at low speed or until oatmeal is well mixed into filling.
Unbaked 9-inch pie shells	6		5. Pour one-sixth (about 2⅔ cups) of the filling into each pie shell. 6. Bake 45 minutes or until center is firm. 7. Serve pie at room temperature cutting each pie into 8 wedges.

DIETARY INFORMATION:
May be used as written for general, high-fiber, bland, soft, and mild 2- to 3-gram sodium-restricted diets.

NOTES: This recipe won a blue ribbon for Shari Burke, the 1976 Pork Queen of Fayette County, Iowa when she entered it in the *1976 Bake It With Lard* contest sponsored by the local branch of the Porkettes.

SHOOFLY PIE
(Pennsylvania Dutch)

YIELD: 48 portions (six 9-inch pies)
PAN SIZE: 9-inch pie pans
PORTION SIZE: 1/8 pie
TEMPERATURE: 350°F Oven

INGREDIENTS	WEIGHTS/MEASURES	FOR ____	METHOD
Sifted all-purpose flour Brown sugar Butter or margarine Salt	2¼ quarts 1½ quarts 3 cups (1 pound 8 ounces) 1½ teaspoons		1. Place flour, sugar, butter, or margarine, and salt in mixer bowl. Mix at low speed for about 2 minutes or until mixture forms coarse crumbs. Do not overmix to form a solid mass.
Baking soda Hot water Light molasses	1 tablespoon 1 quart 1 quart		2. Dissolve soda in water. Add to molasses. Stir to blend.
Unbaked 9-inch pie shells	6		3. Pour one-sixth (about 1¼ cups) of the liquid filling into each pie shell. Sprinkle liquid with one-sixth (about 3¼ cups) of the crumb mixture being careful not to pile the crumbs over the edge of the crust. The crust should be built up around the edges because the filling puffs as it bakes. 4. Bake 30 to 40 minutes or until filling is set. 5. Serve pie at room temperature, cutting each pie into 8 wedges.

DIETARY INFORMATION:

May be used as written for general, bland, soft, and mild 2- to 3-gram sodium-restricted diets.

SWEET POTATO PIE
(Southern)

YIELD: 48 portions (six 10-inch pies)
PAN SIZE: 10-inch pie pans
PORTION SIZE: 1/8 pie
TEMPERATURE: 400°, 325°, and 350°F Oven

INGREDIENTS	WEIGHTS/MEASURES	FOR _____	METHOD
Brown sugar Salt Ground cinnamon	3 cups 1 tablespoon 2 tablespoons		1. Put brown sugar, salt, and cinnamon in mixer bowl. Mix 1/2 minute at low speed to blend.
Mashed or cooked and sieved sweet potatoes Egg yolks Evaporated milk Mapelene flavoring Water	3 quarts (1 No. 10 can) 1 1/2 cups (about 18 medium) 1 1/2 quarts 1/4 cup 3 cups		2. Add potatoes, egg yolks, milk, flavoring, and water to brown sugar mixture. Mix at medium speed about 2 minutes or until well blended.
Unbaked 10-inch pie shells	6		3. Bake unfilled pie shells 5 minutes at 400°F. Pour one-sixth (about 4 1/2 cups) of the filling into each of the warm pie shells. 4. Bake 50 minutes at 325°F or until a silver knife comes out clean from the center of the pie. Cool to room temperature.
Red current or other tart jelly	2 cups		5. Spread a thin layer of jelly using 1/3 cup jelly per pie over the pie filling. Avoid spreading the jelly closer than one half inch to the edge of the crust.
Egg whites Sugar Salt	2 cups (about 18 medium) 2 1/4 cups 1 teaspoon		6. Beat egg whites and cream of tartar together at high speed for about 2 minutes or until foamy. Add sugar, a little at a time, while beating at medium speed for about 6 minutes or until

(Continued)

INGREDIENTS	WEIGHTS/MEASURES	FOR_____	METHOD
Cream of tartar Vanilla	1 teaspoon 1 tablespoon		meringue holds its shape. Add salt and vanilla and beat only until blended. 7. Spread one-sixth of the meringue on top of each pie so that the top of each pie is completely covered and the meringue is touching the pie crust at all edges. 8. Bake at 350°F for 16 to 20 minutes or until meringue is browned. 9. Serve pie at room temperature, cutting each pie into 8 wedges.

DIETARY INFORMATION:

May be used as written for general, high-fiber, soft, bland, and mild 2- to 3-gram sodium-restricted diets.

NOTES: This recipe was furnished by Pauline Lalande, a consulting dietition from Lafayette, Louisiana, who says she cannot take credit for it because several people worked on it including Lois Rivers and her Food and Nutrition class at the University of Southwestern Louisiana.

BAKED INDIAN PUDDING
(New England)

YIELD: 24 portions (1 pan)
PAN SIZE: Heavy double boiler with 6-quart insert
12 × 20 × 2-inch steam table pan

PORTION SIZE: 1 square
TEMPERATURE: 350°F Oven

INGREDIENTS	WEIGHTS/MEASURES	FOR _____	METHOD
Hot water Nonfat dry milk	1 gallon 5½ cups		1. Place water in top of double boiler over slowly simmering water. Stir dry milk into water.
Cornmeal	1⅓ cups		2. Stir cornmeal into hot milk. Cook over simmering water, stirring occasionally, for 20 minutes. Remove from heat.
Molasses Brown sugar Eggs Softened margarine Raisins Ground cinnamon Ground nutmeg Salt	2 cups 2 cups 1½ cups (7 to 8 medium) ½ cup (1 stick) 1 quart 4 teaspoons 2 teaspoons 2 teaspoons		3. Combine molasses, brown sugar, eggs, margarine, raisins, cinnamon, nutmeg, and salt and stir into cornmeal mixture. Mix well and pour into buttered steam table pan.
Cold milk Lemon sauce, whipped topping, cream, or ice cream	1 quart As desired		4. Pour cold milk carefully over pudding. DO NOT MIX MILK INTO PUDDING. 5. Bake 1 hour. Cut 4 × 6 and serve warm or at room temperature with lemon sauce, whipped topping, cream, or ice cream.

DIETARY INFORMATION:

May be used as written for general, high-fiber, and bland diets.

OZARK PUDDING
(Missouri)

YIELD: 48 portions (2 pans)
PAN SIZE: 11 × 14-inch pudding pans
PORTION SIZE: 1 square
TEMPERATURE: 350°F Oven

INGREDIENTS	WEIGHTS/MEASURES	FOR ___	METHOD
Eggs Sugar Vanilla	2 cups (10 medium) 2¼ cups 2 tablespoons		1. Beat eggs at medium speed for 2 minutes. Add sugar and vanilla and beat 1 more minute.
All-purpose flour Baking powder Salt	3 cups ¼ cup 2 teaspoons		2. Stir flour, baking powder, and salt together to blend. Add to sugar mixture and beat at medium speed for 1 minute or until smooth and blended. Do not overbeat.
Cored and diced baking apples Chopped walnuts	3 quarts (4 to 5 pounds) 2 cups		3. Stir apples and nuts into batter. Spread one half (about 2 quarts) of the batter evenly in each of 2 buttered pudding pans. 4. Bake 50 to 55 minutes. Cut each pan 4 × 6.
Vanilla ice cream, coffee cream, whipped cream, or whipped topping	As necessary		5. Serve pudding warm topped with ice cream, coffee cream, whipped cream, or whipped topping.

DIETARY INFORMATION:
May be used as written for general, high-fiber, and mild 2- to 3-gram sodium-restricted diets.

NOTES: Black walnuts are used in Missouri and other parts of the Midwest, but English walnuts may be used if necessary.

RAISIN NUT PUDDING CAKE
(Midwestern)

YIELD: 32 portions (1 pan)
PAN SIZE: 12 × 20 × 2-inch steam table pan
PORTION SIZE: 1 square
TEMPERATURE: 350°F Oven

INGREDIENTS	WEIGHTS/MEASURES	FOR ___	METHOD
All-purpose flour Sugar Baking powder Salt	3½ cups 1 quart 2 tablespoons 1 teaspoon		1. Place flour, sugar, baking powder, and salt together in mixer bowl. Beat at low speed for 1 minute to blend.
Milk Washed and drained raisins Chopped walnuts	2 cups 1 quart 2 cups		2. Add milk, raisins, and nuts to flour mixture. Mix at low speed only until flour is moistened. Spread batter evenly in buttered steam table pan.
Brown sugar Margarine Boiling water Vanilla ice cream, whipped cream, or whipped topping	1 quart 2 tablespoons 1½ quarts As desired		3. Dissolve brown sugar and margarine in boiling water. Pour carefully over batter. DO NOT MIX TOGETHER. 4. Bake 35 to 45 minutes or until cake springs back when touched in the center. 5. Cut warm pudding 4 × 8 and serve with a topping of ice cream, whipped cream, or whipped topping.

DIETARY INFORMATION:

May be used as written for general and high-fiber diets.

INDEX

Acadiana–Cajun
    chicken-sausage gumbo, 74
    dirty rice, 79
    giblet jambalaya, 85
    shrimp etouffée, 91
Adapting recipes, 11
Apple nut squares, 173
Applesauce cookies, 183
Applesauce graham cake, 174
Argo meat loaf, 57
Arkansas
    cornbread, 108
Avocado green salad, 125

Baked bean soup, 22
Baked brown bread, 97
Baked Indian pudding, 207
Baking powder biscuits, 98
Barbecued chicken, 70
Beans
    baked, 144, 145
    frijole salad, 132
    lima bean salad, 134
    plain refried, 147
    refried, 147
    red and rice, 146
    soup, 24
Beef pasties, 42
Biscuit rolls, 99
Black-eyed peas with rice, 153
Boiled dinner, 44
Boston baked beans, 145

Bran
    dark raisin loaves, 102
    dark raisin muffins, 102
    light muffins, 101
    nut coffee cake, 100
    rolls, 103
Breads, 95–114
Bread dressing, 169
Broiled lamb patties, 64
Brown bread, 97
Brown gravy, 167
Brunswick stew, 71
Buttercream frosting, 181

Cabbage
    cole slaw, 128
    molded cole slaw, 129
    spicy cabbage, 149
    with hot vinegar dressing, 148
Cakes and cookies, 171–188
California
    avocado green salad, 125
    chocolate chip date cake, 175
    pork chops in apricot sauce, 67
Can sizes, 16
Caraway noodles, 118
Carrot and cabbage slaw, 128
Catfish gumbo, 26
Celery slaw, 127
Chess pie, 198
Cheese sauce, 165
Chicago
    chili, 46
    chili-mac, 47
    chili with rice, 47
Chicken and sauerkraut, 73
Chicken
    gravy, 167
    gumbo soup, 27

Chicken (*cont'd*)
    sausage gumbo, 74
    spaghetti, 76
    vega, 77
Chili, 46–49
Chocolate
    buttercream frosting, 181
    chip date cake, 175
    chip peanut butter cookies, 184
    fudge brownies, 185
    fudge frosting, 182
    nut frosting, 182
    pecan pie, 202
    rum frosting, 182
Cinnamon crunch cake, 176
Cinnamon rolls, 105
Cinnamon raisin rolls, 106
Clam chowder, 29, 30
Cole slaw, 128
Cornbread dressing, 170
Corn fritters, 109
Cornmeal
    bread, 107, 108
    fried mush, 116
    hush puppies, 110
    Indian pudding, 207
    muffins, 108
    mush, 116
    spoonbread, 114
Country style chicken, 78
Cracklin' bread, 107
Cranberry cheese pie, 200
Cranberry relish, 130
Cream gravy, 167
Cream sauce, 164
Creamy salmon chowder, 37
Creamy split pea soup, 36
Creole
    macaroni, 51
    shrimp, 89

Creole (cont'd)
   sauce, 90
Crisp spice cookies, 188
Cucumber lettuce salad, 131

Dark raisin bran loaves, 102
Dark raisin bran muffins, 102
Date bran muffins, 101
Decreasing a recipe, 10
Deep fat fried chitterlings, 65
Deep fried corn on the cob, 150
Dehydrated onions, 14
Dehydrated peppers, 14
Dietary information, 2
Dipper sizes, 17
Dirty rice, 79

Egg sauce, 165
Enchiladas, 53
Equivalent measures, 12
Escalloped dishes
   apples, 143
   chicken and dressing, 81
   potatoes, 154

Fish, 87–94
Florida
   celery slaw, 127
Fricassee sauce, 165
Fried dishes
   chicken, 83
   cornmeal mush, 116
   hominy grits, 117
   okra, 152
Frosted cookies, 186
Frostings, 181, 182
Frijole salad, 132
Fruit rice, 121

General information, 10

Giblet gravy, 167
Giblet jambalaya, 85
Gingerbread, 178
Golden tuna and noodles, 93
Graham cracker crust, 196
Graham pie crust, 194
Grated potato salad, 136
Guacamole, 126

Ham loaf, 66
Homemade noodles, 119
Hominy grits, 117
Horseradish sauce, 165
Horseradish whipped cream sauce, 166
Hot spiced corned beef sandwich, 50
Hush puppies, 110

Increasing recipes, 10
Indian pudding, 207
Introduction, 1

Jefferson Davis pie, 201
Jewel cookies, 186

Ladle sizes, 17
Lamb patties, 64
Lentil soup, 31
Lettuce
   cucumber salad, 131
   wilted, 133
Light bran muffins, 101
Lima bean salad, 134
Lima bean soup, 23
Louisiana
   catfish gumbo, 26
   Creole sauce, 90
   Creole shrimp, 89
   okra and tomato gumbo, 33
   zucchini in Creole sauce, 159

Manhattan
   clam chowder, 29
Margarine cookies, 186
Margarine pie crust, 193
Martha's company casserole, 55
Maryland
   country style chicken, 78
Mashed potatoes, 155
Measures, 17
Meat loaf, 56, 57
Meats, 39–68
Menudo, 32
Menus, 18
Meringue, 197
Midwestern
   applesauce cookies, 183
   baked beans, 144
   bean soup, 24
   cucumber lettuce salad, 131
   escalloped chicken and dressing, 81
   grated potato salad, 136
   hot spiced corned beef sandwich, 50
   macaroni slaw, 135
   meat loaf, 57
   mock pecan pie, 203
   molasses cookies, 187
   molded strawberries and cream cheese, 138
   potato soup, 35
   raisin nut pudding cake, 209
   wilted lettuce, 133
Minnesota
   caraway noodles, 118
Missouri
   Ozark pudding, 208
Mock pecan pie, 203
Molasses cookies, 187
Molded dishes
   cole slaw, 129

Molded dishes (cont'd)
    rainbow cake, 179
    strawberries and cream cheese, 138
Mustard sauce, 165

Natural pan gravy, 168
New England
    baked beans, 145
    baked bean soup, 22
    baked brown bread, 97
    baked Indian pudding, 207
    boiled dinner, 44
    Boston baked beans, 145
    clam chowder, 30
    corn muffins, 108
    cornmeal mush, 116
    cranberry cheese pie, 200
    cranberry relish, 130
    crisp spice cookies, 188
    fried cornmeal mush, 116
    oyster stew, 34
Nonfat dry milk, 13
Noodles
    caraway, 118
    homemade, 119
Northern Michigan
    beef pasties, 42
Northwestern
    creamy salmon chowder, 37
Nut bran muffins, 101

Okra and tomato gumbo, 33
Onion gravy, 167
Onion rolls, 111
Orange buttercream frosting, 181
Oyster stew, 34
Ozark pudding, 208

Pan sizes, 11
Pecan pie, 202
Pecan rolls, 106
Pennsylvania Dutch
    cabbage and hot vinegar dressing, 148
    shoofly pie, 204
    snickerdoodle coffee cake, 113
    wilted lettuce, 133
Pies and puddings, 189–209
Pie crust, 191
Pineapple glazed yams, 157
Plain refried beans, 147
Pork chops in apricot sauce, 67
Potatoes
    mashed, 155
    escalloped, 154
    grated salad, 136
    soup, 35
    substitutes, 115–122

Raisins
    bran muffins, 101
    glazed yams, 158
    nut pudding cake, 209
Raspberry devil's food cake, 180
Red beans and rice, 146
Refried beans, 147
Reuben sandwich, 58
Rice
    fruit, 121
    steamed, 122
    with black-eyed peas, 153
Roast beef hash, 59

Salads, 123–139
Salad dressing for vegetables, 139
Salmon pâté, 88
Sauces, gravies, and dressings, 163–170
Sauerkraut salad, 137

Sauerkraut with tomatoes, 156
Shoofly pie, 204
Shrimp Creole, 89
Shrimp etouffée, 91
Simmered dishes
    chitterlings, 65
    greens, 151
    pigs' feet, 68
    pork hocks, 68
Snickerdoodle coffee cake, 113
Soups, 21–38
Southern
    black-eyed peas with rice, 153
    Brunswick stew, 71
    catfish gumbo, 26
    chicken gumbo soup, 27
    cornbread, 107
    cornbread dressing, 170
    cracklin' bread, 107
    Creole macaroni, 51
    fried chicken, 83
    fried hominy grits, 117
    fried okra, 152
    hominy grits, 117
    hush puppies, 110
    Jefferson Davis pie, 201
    pecan pie, 202
    red beans and rice, 146
    simmered greens, 151
    spoonbread, 114
    sweet potato pie, 205
Southwestern
    enchiladas, 53
    frijole salad, 132
    guacamole, 126
    menudo, 32
    plain refried beans, 147
    refried beans, 147
    steak ranchero, 61

Southwestern (*cont'd*)
    tacos, 62
    tostados, 63
Spicy cabbage, 149
Spoonbread, 114
Steak ranchero, 61
Steamed rice, 122
Supreme sauce, 165
Sweet potato pie, 205

Tacos, 62
Texas
    chicken spaghetti, 76
    chili, 48
    chess pie, 198
Tomato bouillon, 38
Tomato gravy, 167
Tostados, 63
Turkey gravy, 167

Vegetables, 141–161
Vegetable gravy, 167

Western
    lentil soup, 31
White sauce, 164
Wilted lettuce, 133

Yankee
    cornbread, 108
    corn muffins, 108

Zucchini in Creole sauce, 159

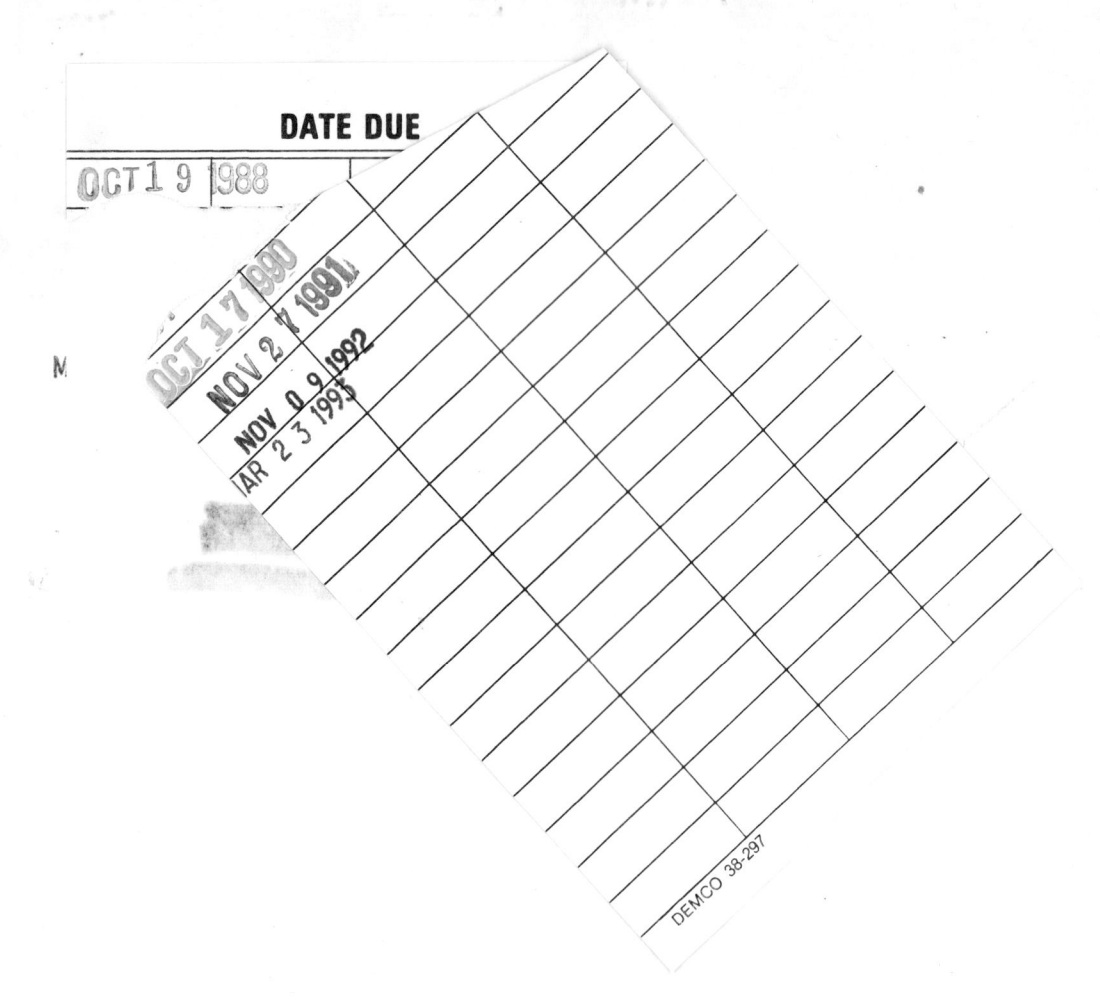

DATE DUE			
OCT 19 1988			
OCT 17 1990			
NOV 27 1991			
NOV 0 9 1992			
AR 2 3 1993			

DEMCO 38-297